THE NETHERLANDS INTERNATIONAL DIRECT INVESTMENT POSITION

Marius van Nieuwkerk and Robert P. Sparling

The Netherlands international direct investment position

Monetary Monographs No. 4

1985 De Nederlandsche Bank n.v.
Martinus Nijhoff Publishers, Dordrecht

ISBN 90-247-3330-8

Distributors
For the United States and Canada: Kluwer Academic Publishers,
190 Old Derby Street, Hingham MA 02043, USA
For the UK and Ireland: Kluwer Academic Publishers, MTP Press Limited, Falcon House,
Queen Square, Lancaster LA1 1RN, England
For all other countries: Kluwer Academic Publishers Group, Distribution Centre,
P.O. Box 322, 3300 AH Dordrecht, The Netherlands

Printed in The Netherlands

Contents

Foreword

For the Netherlands, commercial and cultural contacts across the borders are of vital importance. The world's eighth trading nation holding pride of place in many market segments, the Netherlands is highly dependent on developments worldwide. Through other economic ties as well, our country is firmly embedded in the world around us.

Until the Second World War, the methods used in the Netherlands to collect data about these international relations were less than adequate. As a result, the compilation of a consistent overview in the form of a balance of payments was barely feasible in those years. After the War this situation was improved markedly, and the Bank was assigned a key role in the compilation of the balance of payments.

This role entails that the Bank must also answer the many requests for information about the underlying data and that, by analysis of these data, it must come to policy recommendations. It is our experience – almost daily – that international direct investment is among the subjects which have been attracting major attention in recent years, both at home and abroad.

The present monograph of the Bank's Balance-of-Payments Department seeks to meet this need for information, and also highlights some backgrounds to the underlying data. The Bank's statutory duty to maintain the confidentiality of data of individual enterprises and institutions imposes restrictions and in a number of cases necessitated the combination of data by sector and/or country. Notably for Netherlands outward direct investment, this duty is of major significance, as a relatively small number of large enterprises accounts for a very substantial part of total outward investment. In this context I wish to mention industry's generous cooperation in furnishing the requested data every year and its willingness to elucidate backgrounds. It is this cooperation which has made this monograph possible.

W.F. Duisenberg
President

Preface

The present study is largely based on the results of a survey which was set up in the early 1970s by C. Bakker and P. Speelman, who were then in charge of the Bank's Balance-of-Payments Department. Later, the implementation was notably the responsibility of A.L. Oskam. From the very start, the organization of the survey was such that hardly any subsequent adaptation has been required to meet the often strongly changing purposes of international reporting and analysis.

The compilation, processing and analysis of the data have made heavy demands on the staff of the Administration & Control and Statistical Analysis sectors of the Balance-of-Payments Department. I owe a debt of gratitude to them all. I am also indebted to Ms. H.M. de Jong, N.P. Driesprong, J.C.F. Versluis and my co-author R.P. Sparling for their contributions to this monograph. Finally, for the discussions about the international reconciliation of investment statistics, I thank my fellow-members of the 'IMF Working Party on the Statistical Discrepancy in World Current Account Balances', a group of experts which was installed in early January 1985 by IMF Managing Director De Larosière to trace the causes of international balance-of-payments discrepancies.

November 1985 M. van Nieuwkerk

1 Introduction and summary

The Netherlands has long been familiar with the phenomenon of direct investment abroad. Apart from colonial ties, the West-Indische Compagnie's acquisition in 1626 of the Manhattan peninsula in exchange for guns, bullets and ironmongery – representing a total value of sixty guilders – is perhaps to be regarded as one of the first instances of Netherlands direct investment abroad. Yet, for a very long time, this 'active' form of investing abroad played only a secondary role in the traditionally voluminous capital exports from the Netherlands. For a number of centuries, the Netherlands suppliers of capital preferred the more 'passive' form of investment in foreign financial assets.

It was only at the beginning of this century that this pattern began to change as Netherlands enterprises increasingly acquired lasting direct holdings in existing enterprises abroad or set up subsidiaries abroad. This may be illustrated by some figures on the composition and development of Netherlands investment in the United States. Whereas round the turn of the century direct investment accounted for less than 10 % of the total Netherlands investment position in the United States, in the 1930s this share had increased to nearly one-third.[1] Thus, at that time, the Netherlands had already become the *third* largest foreign investor in the United States, after the United Kingdom and Canada.

The years following the Second World War saw a continuation of this shift from 'passive' external investment towards more 'active' forms of external investment. This development was so marked that, ever since, Netherlands external security transactions have yielded a net inflow of capital, after having led to net outflows for a number of centuries.[2]

This monograph focuses on Netherlands outward and inward direct investment, and more in particular on the external direct investment position in recent years. The external direct investment *flows* have been recorded in the Netherlands balance of payments since 1947; additionally, since 1973, data have been collected by means of surveys on the direct investment *positions* of Netherlands enterprises abroad and of foreign enterprises in the Netherlands. The results of these surveys of direct investment positions provide a most valuable additional insight into the wealth positions

---

1 K.D. Bosch, *De Nederlandse beleggingen in de Verenigde Staten,* Amsterdam, 1948.

2 Van Nieuwkerk *et al., External security transactions of the Netherlands,* De Nederlandsche Bank N.V., Reprint No.118, 1984.

resulting from the direct investment flows, and permit further information to be derived about the movements in the rates of return on such investment. Furthermore, the data permit sectoral breakdowns, although the specification to be published is limited by the statutory confidentiality of the data obtained from the individual enterprises included in the surveys. This applies notably to the Netherlands figures, because the foreign direct investment position of the Netherlands is heavily dominated by some large multinational enterprises: nearly three-quarters of the Netherlands direct investment position abroad is accounted for by the ten largest multinational enterprises.

This monograph first deals with some aspects of the theoretical background to international direct investment. Subsequently, developments in the Netherlands are discussed, and the results of the surveys are presented, broken down by sector, by country and by sector/country. The *conclusions* can be summarized as follows:

A Outward direct investment

1. Viewed within the total of Netherlands cross-border transactions, direct investment is of major significance. According to the surveys conducted, the direct investment position abroad amounted to Fl. 120 billion at end-1983, so that the Netherlands ranked third among the world's direct investors, after the United States and the United Kingdom. Furthermore, the data show that the Netherlands had remained the third largest direct investor in the United States, after the United Kingdom and Canada.

   For the period 1973-1978, the surveys show a growth of over Fl. 75 billion in the direct investment position. Nearly two-thirds of this increase resulted from capital exports from the Netherlands, while the rest ensued from retention of profits by foreign subsidiaries. The growth of the outstanding amount averaged 11 % per annum, roughly the same as the average increase in the value of exports in the same period.

   The rate of return on outward investment was nearly 10% per annum; however, this percentage masks wide differences among the various groups of countries and the various sectors. The rate of return on direct investment in the United States averaged twice that in Europe, while that on direct investment in the countries of Southeast Asia was three times as high. Furthermore, in the oil and chemical industries, the rate of return was substantially higher than in the metal industry and in services; however, it must be noted with regard to services that the rate was depressed by initial costs in respect of recent investment.
2. Until recently, outward direct investment was accounted for almost entirely by the production industries. Recently, however, a significant shift towards services has been discernible, a development which has been accompanied by the evolu-

tion of a considerable number of national enterprises in the services sector into full-fledged multinationals. This suggests that the future of the Netherlands economy must be expected to be marked by increasing orientation towards services, nationally and internationally (section 7.1.1).

Geographically, the United States in particular has gained popularity among Netherlands direct investors, who have tended to shift attention away from Europe. Factors adversely affecting direct investment in Europe have included market saturation and comparatively low rates of return. The absence of a homogeneous European market, where costs would be lower and the opportunities for product development would be much better than on the present fragmented markets, would appear to be among the principal causes of these comparative disadvantages (sections 6.1.1 and 6.1.2). In addition to direct investment in the United States, Netherlands direct investment in the NICs (Newly Industrializing Countries) also showed a very marked growth, centring on the developing countries in Asia. Here, too, relatively high rates of return and well developed markets would appear to exert a major attraction. However, the share of the other developing countries in total Netherlands outward direct investment declined (section 6.1.4).

3. The future may probably be expected to see a wide-ranging continuation of the expansion of Netherlands outward direct investment. Whereas in 1984 capital outflows consequent on direct investment totalled at least Fl. 8.5 billion, the recorded outflow in the twelve-month period up to and including June 1985 came to Fl. 10.5 billion (the amount of retained profits for this period is not yet known). On the one hand, the domestic 'propelling forces' in the Netherlands – in the form of healthy large enterprises having ownership-specific advantages which they wish to use across the borders as well – are strong and now also extend to the services sector. On the other hand, the 'pulling forces' are likewise strong, especially the location advantages elsewhere as reflected in market size and market homogeneity. Furthermore, advantages in terms of return rates and costs offered by locations abroad may continue to exert a pulling force.

   Considering this, prospects would appear to be for increasing specialization along the lines of the comparative advantages of each individual country. In this light, cross-border direct investment may be expected to complement rather than replace national investment. This is probably so already to a large extent. For instance, the employment offered in the Netherlands by large Netherlands-based multinational enterprises would appear to have developed less unfavourably than that of nationally oriented Netherlands enterprises, despite continuing outward direct investment.

B Inward direct investment

4. Until the Second World War, foreign direct investment in the Netherlands was presumably of relatively minor significance. It was only in the 1950s and 1960s that the Netherlands experienced a wave of inward direct investment, originating notably from the United States as well as from neighbouring countries. The results of the surveys for the period 1973-1983 show that, at Fl. 52 billion, the outstanding nominal amount of foreign direct investment in the Netherlands in 1983 was two-and-a-half times that in 1973. Here, too, nearly two-thirds of the increase was accounted for by capital flows and the rest by retained profits. Average growth in nominal terms was slightly below that recorded for outward direct investment. It was also below the nominal growth of Netherlands imports in the period concerned.

5. Averaging 11.5 %, the rate of return on foreign direct investment in the Netherlands was slightly above that on Netherlands outward direct investment. Again, this average is seen to mask wide differences, which become apparent from a breakdown by country of investment origin. For instance, subsidiaries of US enterprises achieved rates of 19 %, against an average of 6 % for subsidiaries of enterprises based in the EC. Apparently, in the interests of their shareholders, the US enterprises demand higher rates of return on investment than do their European-based counterparts. Presumably, they are able to do so because their opportunities of using their homogeneous domestic market as a launching pad for new products – and of withdrawing to home base if they prove unsuccessful elsewhere – are much greater than for European-based enterprises, albeit possibly at the expense of their geographical distribution (section 6.2.5).

6. During the period concerned, inward direct investment was increasingly oriented towards Netherlands service enterprises: in 1983 the share of services was as high as over 40 %, against over a quarter in 1973. Viewed geographically, especially the non-EC countries, notably the United States, were major investors. Here, too, prospects are for increasing interwovenness, in terms of trade and investment, between the Netherlands economy and the economies of other countries. The Netherlands offers foreign investors a number of distinct advantages (section 7.1.2). Moreover, a study conducted by the University of Utrecht has shown that the development of employment in Netherlands subsidiaries of foreign enterprises compares very favourably with the development of overall employment in the Netherlands. More generally, this study has revealed that 'foreign operations in the Netherlands represent a relatively strong element of the Netherlands economy and may hold out important prospects for future developments'.

2 A country's direct investment position

2.1 Propensity to invest

Within the body of modern theory on international direct investment, a prominent place is held by the works of Dunning, who has attempted to explain the international direct investment position of various countries.[3]

Dunning holds that the propensity to invest abroad depends upon the following three factors:

a. The degree to which enterprises in a country possess 'assets' or rights which other – foreign – enterprises do not possess or cannot acquire, at least not on the same conditions. Dunning calls these 'assets' *ownership-specific* advantages to the extent that they are proprietary and are fully or partially transferrable across national borders. Cases in point are superior technology (whether or not embodied in specific products) and superior marketing techniques leading to product differentiation.

b. The degree to which it is profitable for enterprises to effect intra-group exploitation of such advantages (*internalization* of advantages). Cases in point are intra-group technical service agreements and management contracts, but also joint operations of parent and subsidiary.

c. The degree to which enterprises consider it profitable to locate any part of their production facilities outside their home countries. This will depend on the attractions of *location-specific* advantages.

Table 1 shows a schematic representation of the various options open to an entrepreneur to exploit the advantages.

Possession of ownership advantages is a major condition for international production and/or sales. The availability of profitable opportunities for internalization may prompt an enterprise to opt for investing in and exporting to other countries, in preference to transferring proprietary know-how. Location advantages play a role in the choice between investing abroad and exporting; examples are relative costs, the availability of certain natural resources, but also import duties or quotas.

In the Netherlands literature it has been noted that, in addition to these three – more or less objective – factors, two other factors exert an influence on the development of an enterprise's international direct investment.[4]

---

[3] John H. Dunning, *Explaining the international direct investment position of countries: towards a dynamic or developmental approach,* Weltwirtschaftliches Archiv, Heft 1, 1981, pp. 30-64.

[4] J.E. Andriessen, Multinationale ondernemingen, and H.W. de Jong, De internationalisatie van het Nederlandse bedrijfsleven, both in *'Ondernemen in Nederland'*, Kluwer, Deventer, 1985.

Table 1
Options open to enterprises to gain access to foreign markets

Advantages	Mechanism		
	Direct investment	Exports	Transfer of know-how
Ownership	yes	yes	yes
Internalization	yes	yes	no
Location	yes	no	no

These are, on the one hand, *subjective* factors such as the will to expand and the readiness to take risks and, on the other, the *development stage of the market.*[5]
A more detailed discussion is contained in Chapter 3, where these five aspects are highlighted against the background of the Netherlands situation.

2.2 Direct investment position

The very variety of these factors and their different weights in the various countries stand in the way of an exact and clear-cut explanation of the international direct investment flows. Yet, at the macro-economic level, some common tendencies may be distilled. Dunning, for example, points to the relationship between a country's net external direct investment position – defined as the difference between the country's outward and inward direct investment – and the country's 'development stage'. He distinguishes four such stages.

At the *first stage,* the net investment position is nil or slightly negative, meaning that inward direct investment exceeds outward direct investment. Generally, there is barely any inward direct investment, if at all, as the location advantages are negligible. Additionally, the country itself undertakes no outward direct investment owing either to a lack of ownership advantages or to the fact that others are better positioned to exploit them. An example is the group of the poorest developing countries, with small markets, a background domestic structure, a low-skilled population, etc.

At the *second stage,* the net direct investment position is negative and the gap between inward and outward direct investment is widening. Inward investment expands owing to location advantages such as market growth, stimulation of import substitution, exploitation of natural resources and cheap labour. Examples are

[5] At the macro-economic level, Dunning has made a division into growth stages to explain a country's direct investment position, which may be viewed as the macro-economic equivalent of the development stage of the market (section 2.2).

densely populated and advancing developing countries such as Brazil, India and Malaysia. Outward direct investment is still insubstantial as the incentives offered by ownership advantages, if any, are still weak.

At the *third stage,* the net direct investment position is still negative, but the gap between inward and outward direct investment is narrowing. The rate of inward direct investment is weakening, for instance because initial ownership advantages are eroding and/or the location advantages offered to foreign multinational enterprises are lessening (emergence of competitive national industries, rising costs, reduced growth due to saturation, etc.). On the other hand, outward direct investment is increasing as national industries are acquiring ownership advantages which they wish to exploit internationally to benefit from location advantages abroad.

At the *fourth stage,* outward direct investment exceeds inward direct investment, so that the net direct investment position is positive. This position reflects strong ownership advantages and an increasing tendency on the part of domestic enterprises to exploit these advantages abroad under their own auspices. This tendency to internalize these advantages is attended by growing geographical diversification of the multinational enterprise, and may lead to intra-group regional and/or product specialization.

At the heart of this division into stages is the assumption of a relationship between a country's net direct investment position and the degree of its economic development. This division is, of course, a highly stylized representation of reality and deviations from this pattern are not difficult to point out. Compare, for instance, the difference between countries having abundant natural resources and those lacking them, and the difference in 'maturity' between the production industries sector and that of the services sector in some countries. It is clear, however, that after the Second World War most Western European countries have evolved from the third stage – *le défi américain* – to the fourth. In the Federal Republic of Germany, for example; the period until the mid-1970s was marked virtually throughout by net inflows of direct investment, a situation which has been the reverse ever since.

3 The development in the Netherlands

3.1 Background

The five factors listed above are indubitably perceivable in the operations of many Netherlands multinational enterprises, albeit with the nuances peculiar to each enterprise and each country. Thus, with regard to the factors concerning the development stage of the market and the will to expand or the readiness to take risks, it might be noted that the Netherlands is a small country with a traditionally very open economy. As a result, undertaking operations abroad was not only usual, it was a vital condition for any Netherlands entrepreneur wishing to operate on a significant scale. This could be a factor underlying the traditionally stronger drive towards international expansion evinced by Netherlands enterprises compared to their German and French counterparts.

The history of Netherlands multinational enterprises also shows that Netherlands entrepreneurs have certainly not been lacking in readiness to take risks, taking on their competitors at the latter's home base. Thus, as early as in 1908, the oil industry held that – if competitors were 'to be taught once and for all not to disturb the peace' – it had itself to undertake production of the traded oil (which underlay the strength of the domestic industry) in the oil fields in the United States.[6] In 1903, the Netherlands electric-light bulb industry did not flinch from taking on its biggest competitor at his own home base, Berlin, causing the existing sales cartel to be broken. A much more recent example of the combination of the drive towards international expansion and the willingness to take risks is afforded by the take-overs of US insurance companies by Netherlands insurance groups; these take-overs established the foundations for the ultimate success of the internationalization efforts and were attended by the emergence of new multinationals in this area.

Not surprisingly, the internationally operating Netherlands enterprises are characterized by a traditionally high degree of multinationalization, as evident from, among other things, the various countries of establishment and the internationalization of top management.[7] In all interesting markets, Netherlands enterprises wish to be both present and at home, and this is no longer confined to enterprises from the production industries, but is also increasingly true of enterprises from the services sector, such as trading and retail trading, banking and insurance, publishing and information services.

---

[6] Bosch, *op. cit.*

[7] See both Andriessen and De Jong, *op. cit.*

Apart from the drive towards cross-border growth and development, a key theme in the history of Netherlands multinational enterprises has been the application of proprietary know-how across the boundaries of the domestic markets. Whether in the oil industry, the food industry, the electric-light bulb industry or the rayon industry, the 'constant and continuous blending of the skills of scientist and salesman' was and remains a key factor in the successful operation of the industrial multinational enterprise. The fact that this combination of salesmanship and application of technological know-how is still considered essential is evident from a recent note on the international location policy of the modern electronics industry, which states that 'the geographical location must provide access to the manifestly leading markets and technological centres in the world, that is, both the largest markets in certain sectors in terms of sales volume and the technologically most advanced markets'.[8]

Exploiting better growth opportunities abroad does not, however, always automatically lead to direct investment (Table 1). This is shown by the example of the Netherlands beer industry's exports to the United States. Despite a favourable development of sales in that country, the beer industry continues to prefer to export rather than undertake local production, thus exploiting the advantages of the image of an imported brand. The case of transfer of know-how only is also found in Netherlands practice, for instance, in the car industry for know-how on automatic gear-boxes.

In summary, it may be stated that, considering the fact that the Netherlands accommodates a number of relatively very large multinational enterprises, it may be assumed that the Netherlands has strong ownership advantages and wishes to exploit them on a substantial scale. Moreover, these advantages can be internalized and, hence, there is a major readiness to come to, and accept the risks of, intra-group exploitation of these advantages, whether locally (by means of exports) or across the borders (by means of direct investment). The location advantages would thus appear to be a major factor underlying these entrepreneurial decisions.

3.2 Development

Especially after the turn of the century and more in particular after the First World War, the foundations were laid for many Netherlands multinational enterprises. At the time, capital was increasingly laid out for direct participations and acquisitions, in which a direct and lasting influence was exerted. From the beginning, emphasis was on the production industries, the oil industry holding pride of place. For instance, as early as in 1920 it was noted about the international expansion of the oil industry that 'the value has been clearly shown of production not concentrated in one area but distributed throughout the world, so that distribution can be effected under geographic-

[8] Het Financieele Dagblad, April 26, 1985.

ally favourable conditions. It must be possible for each market to be provided with products from the areas which are best located geographically'. In-house production of the traded oil and the construction of in-house facilities for storage and sale went hand in hand. Especially in the United States a forceful *pénétration pacifique* took place. After the First World War the Netherlands food industry, the rayon industry and the electric-light bulb and radio industry also increasingly set up operations far across the borders. Additionally, the establishment of operations abroad was more and more stimulated by increasing nationalism and protectionism in international trade in the 1920s and 1930s.[9]

An illustration of this early cross-border expansion of Netherlands industry is afforded by developments in the United States. At the end of August 1939, according to data of the US Federal Reserve Board, the Netherlands occupied a very favourable portfolio and direct investment position in the United States, accounting for nearly one-eighth of total foreign holdings (Table 2). As regards both portfolio investment and direct investment, the Netherlands, after the United Kingdom and Canada, was the United States' *third* largest creditor, just ahead of Switzerland. At that time 98.5 % of the Netherlands direct investment position related to investment in the production industries (mainly oil and chemicals) and the remainder to services. The traditionally very strong preference of Netherlands investors for foreign bonds is evident from the fact that in 1939 the Netherlands still ranked prominently *first* among foreign investors in these securities. Yet, long before the Second World War, a distinct shift had already occurred from this 'passive' form of investing to more 'active' ones, such as direct investment.

Thus, in 1939 the share of direct investment in total Netherlands investment in securities and direct investment in the United States was already more than 45 %, above the average recorded for most other countries. Round the turn of the century, this share had been less than 7.5 %, rising to 21 % in 1914 and 36 % in 1919. After the Second World War, this shift towards direct investment persisted.

Compared with this growing outward investment of the Netherlands, pre-War *inward* investment was probably of practically no significance according to US sources.[10] However, these figures are probably not entirely complete. Nevertheless, a recent survey conducted by the Geographical Institute of the University of Utrecht about the year of establishment of foreign enterprises in the Netherlands has also shown that the period up to 1946 was of relatively minor importance.[11] The number of foreign enterprises established in the Netherlands before the Second World War

---

9 Bosch, *op. cit.*

10 Cleona Lewis, *The United States and Foreign Investment Problems,* The Brookings Institution, 1948.

11 *Internationale ondernemingen in Nederland, omvang en lokatie van vestigingen in Nederland,* Geografisch Instituut, Rijksuniverstiteit Utrecht, December 1984.

Table 2
Holdings of dollar balances and investments in the United States, end-August 1939 (millions of dollars)

Country/group of countries	Dollar balances	Marketable securities				'Direct' and 'other invest-ments'	Total
		Total	Ordinary shares	Preferred shares	Bonds		
United Kingdom	595	735	535	120	80	900	2,230
France	315	185	130	15	40	80	580
Canada	355	500	400	60	40	560	1,415
Germany	10	–	–	–	–	–	10
Italy	10	–	–	–	–	–	10
Netherlands	160	470	270	25	175	380	1,010
Switzerland	285	375	295	30	50	170	830
Other European countries	430	130	65	30	35	120	680
Latin America	390	40	30	5	5	10	440
Far East, etc.	355	380	335	20	25	180	915
Total foreign holdings	2,905	2,815	2,060	305	450	2,400	8,120

Source: Federal Reserve Board Bulletin, December 1939; see also Bosch, *op. cit.*

was less than 9 % of the total number of enterprises included in the survey. Even in that period, the United States was already the principal country of origin: nearly 40 % of all enterprises concerned. In addition, the United Kingdom, the Federal Republic of Germany and Switzerland were relatively important countries of origin. In terms of volume, investment in oil and chemicals, food and metals was probably significant, sectors in which Netherlands enterprises also held strong positions.

3.3 Development stages

When the Netherlands situation is viewed in terms of Dunning's division into stages it is, all in all, likely that Netherlands outward direct investment gained some significance round the turn of the century and began to exhibit a strong growth notably after the First World War. Presumably, it exceeded inward direct investment from the very outset. Emphasis was probably almost exclusively on the production industries.

After the Second World War, within the framework of a complete registration of all inward and outward flows for the compilation of the Netherlands balance of payments, investment *flows* have been recorded since 1947 (Chart 1). Until 1959 this flow registration covered only capital participations, that is 'the acquisition of a more or less lasting interest in an enterprise by way of participation in the share capital, with the aim of exercising actual influence on the management of the enterprise'. From that year onwards, the registration was extended to include short and long-term intra-group lending, while since 1968 intra-group current accounts have also been included. Thus, the definition is in conformity with the IMF definitions regarding direct investment, with the exception of the inclusion of retained profits.

The internationally agreed methods for accounting for these retained profits are not uniform for the balance of payments, on the one hand, and the National Accounts, on the other. For various reasons, the Netherlands National Accounts and the Netherlands balance of payments show only the *distributed* part of profits. For details, the reader is referred to Appendices A and B.

As is evident from Chart 1, after the Second World War the outward direct investment flows have exceeded the inward direct investment flows practically throughout. Averaged per annum, capital *outflows* on this account amounted to 1.3 % of national income and capital *inflows* to 0.7 %. In the period 1960-1975, this deficit on the 'direct investment balance' was relatively limited, notably as a result of the strong expansion of foreign direct investment in the Netherlands.

Considering the ratio of outward to inward direct investment flows, it may be expected that the Netherlands direct investment *position* has developed in such a way that the accumulated amount (i.e. the stock) of Netherlands direct investment abroad far exceeds the accumulated amount of foreign direct investment in the Netherlands. This should certainly be true of direct investment in the production industries, as it is this very sector on which the multinationalization of Netherlands enterprises centred until recently.

4 The Netherlands direct investment position, 1973-1983

4.1 Coverage of survey

Data about the Netherlands direct investment position have been compiled since 1973. In 1983 this survey among Netherlands investors abroad and foreign investors in the Netherlands covered nearly 3,500 enterprises, institutions and persons, who together accounted for 7,800 direct investment relationships (Chart 2). Of these enterprises, institutions and persons, 1,200 reported only Netherlands direct investment abroad, involving a total of 3,800 cases of direct investment. The number of economic units which reported only foreign direct investment in the Netherlands was 1,800, accounting for a total of nearly 2,100 cases of direct investment. Those reporting both foreign and Netherlands direct investment totalled 500, involving 1,400 cases of outward direct investment and 600 of inward direct investment.

For 1983 a sample study was made to ascertain the size of the so-called lasting interest, on the basis of which the relationship was reported as direct investment. As is shown in Chart 2, the bulk of direct investment concerned an interest of 75 % or over. The number of cases of direct investment concerning an interest of 50 % or over was more than three-quarters of the total, both for outward and for inward direct investment.

4.2 Direct investment position and rate of return

Between end-1973 and end-1983 the outstanding amount of *Netherlands* direct investment abroad nearly tripled from Fl. 44 billion to Fl. 120 billion. Thus, the Netherlands is among the world's largest direct investors, ranking third, after the United States and the United Kingdom.[12] The growth averaged nearly 11 % per annum; notably the late 1970s saw a growth acceleration, which appears to have been sustained until recently (Chart 3).

In the first half of the period, the growth rate was over 6.5 % and in the second half more than double that percentage (14.5 %). The bulk of this direct investment consists of capital participations. The rate of return on these participations in the period 1974-1983 fluctuated around an average of over 10 %. A breakdown by country and by sector reveals much wider fluctuations (Chapter 5 and 6). The share of intra-group

---

[12] J.M. Stopford and J.H. Dunning, *Multinationals, company performance and global trends*, London, 1983.

loans and intra-group current accounts in total direct investment at end-1983 was over 16 %. Interest rates on these loans and accounts averaged 5.5 %, with relatively minor fluctuations. Presumably, this percentage is used as an intra-group settlement rate. The overall rate of return on Netherlands direct investment abroad thus comes out at an average of 9.5 % (Table 3).

The outstanding amount of *foreign* direct investment in the Netherlands at end-1983 was Fl. 52 billion, less than half the amount of Netherlands direct investment abroad. Not only in absolute terms but also – to a certain extent – in terms of growth, foreign direct investment in the Netherlands lags behind Netherlands direct investment abroad. The total foreign position increased by an annual average of over 9.5 % and has not shown any substantial growth acceleration in recent years: the nominal growth rates were nearly 9 % in the first half of the period concerned, and 10.5 % in the second.

It is noteworthy that, where inward direct investment is concerned, capital participations account for a much smaller share in the total direct investment position: over 70 %, against nearly 85 % for outward direct investment. It is also evident that, at an average of nearly 15 %, the rate of return on foreign enterprises' capital participations in the Netherlands is considerably higher than the corresponding figure for outward direct investment. On the other hand, at an average of 5 %, interest rates on inward investment credits are practically equal to those on outward investment credits, with likewise relatively minor fluctuations. This provides additional support for the impression that this percentage is an intra-group rate.

The substantial difference in return rates on outward and inward capital participations may be due to a number of factors:

a. The difference in the manner of financing such investment. As, compared with outward direct investment, inward direct investment is to a larger extent financed from intra-group loans (bearing a low rate of interest), the overall rates of return on outward and inward direct investment are much more similar (Table 3).

Table 3
Return rates on direct investment
(%)

Description	Outward direct investment			Inward direct investment		
	1974/ 1978	1979/ 1983	1974/ 1983	1974/ 1978	1979/ 1983	1974/ 1983
Capital participations	9.3	11.1	10.2	14.8	14.9	14.8
Loans, etc.	5.5	5.3	5.4	4.5	5.5	5.0
Total	8.7	10.1	9.4	11.1	11.9	11.5

b. Additionally, a role may be played by the fact that, because of the relatively small size of their home market, Netherlands enterprises wishing to expand on a larger scale must resort much more rapidly to investing abroad than foreign enterprises must to investing in the Netherlands.

   Moreover, in the event of setbacks, the latter enterprises have much bigger opportunities for repatriating a major part of their investments to their larger and often more homogeneous home market: 'withdrawal to home base'. This means that the Netherlands needs foreign countries much more than conversely and that, as a consequence, the return rates may differ accordingly (see also section 6.2.5).

c. In connection with the preceding factor, a role is also played by differences in the return rates demanded by investors from the various countries. It is, for instance, well-known that US enterprises demand high rates of return from their subsidiaries, on penalty of close-down or disposal (section 6.2.5).

d. Another factor of significance could be a difference in the degree of 'maturity' between *outward* and *inward* direct investment. This is probably true of the services sector in particular, where the multinationalization of Netherlands enterprises is of relatively recent date compared with that in, for instance, the United States. Consequently, in this sector the return rates on outward direct investment are as yet significantly lower than those on inward direct investment (Chapter 5).

e. A final factor might be found in the decrease in the value of most currencies against the Netherlands guilder during the period concerned. For sterling this decrease averaged 3 %, for the French franc 4.5 %, the Belgian franc 2 % and the Italian lira 8.5 %. (The US dollar increased in value by an average of 1.5 %.) To the extent that profits are expressed in these currencies, conversion into guilders leads to deflation compared with guilder returns on inward investment.

4.3 Changes in direct investment positions and balance-of-payments flows

As noted earlier, the Netherlands balance of payments includes only those amounts that are actually paid or settled (balance of payments on a cash basis). Changes in direct investment consequent on, for example, retained profits lead to differences between balance-of-payments flows and changes in stocks. This also applies, of course, to exchange rate differences and revaluations. Table 4 presents an overview of the various changes.

Column 3 of this Table shows that from 1973 onwards the amount of outward direct investment, increasing by over Fl. 76 billion, tripled to Fl. 120 billion. Two-thirds (Fl. 47.5 billion) of this increase was accounted for by actual direct investment flows, which were entered as such in the balance of payments under direct investment

Table 4
Breakdown of changes in direct investment positions
(millions of guilders)

Year	Position at Jan. 1	Position at Dec. 31	Changes	of which due to:		
				capital flows	retained profits	exchange rate differences, revalutations, etc.
	(1)	(2)	(3)	(4)	(5)	(6)
Netherlands direct investment abroad						
1974	43,699	49,622	5,923	4,224	2,374	-675
1975	49,622	53,561	3,939	3,767	1,248	-1,076
1976	53,561	51,517	-2,044	2,864	2,064	-6,972
1977	51,517	57,805	6,288	3,383	1,781	1,124
1978	57,805	60,572	2,767	2,445	1,057	-735
1979	60,572	71,974	11,402	5,606	5,630	166
1980	71,974	89,685	17,711	6,575	3,431	7,705
1981	89,685	99,508	9,823	8,163	2,223	-563
1982	99,508	104,291	4,783	5,014	1,741	-1,972
1983	104,291	119,886	15,595	5,406	4,241	5,948
Total changes			76,187	47,447	25,790	2,950
Foreign direct investment in the Netherlands						
1974	20,659	23,687	3,028	2,282	379	367
1975	23,687	26,382	2,695	2,269	642	-216
1976	26,382	28,426	2,044	1,192	591	261
1977	28,426	30,179	1,753	449	803	501
1978	30,179	31,565	1,386	1,613	840	-1,067
1979	31,565	36,147	4,582	2,072	1,321	1,189
1980	36,147	40,817	4,670	3,410	508	752
1981	40,817	45,432	4,615	3,160	613	842
1982	45,432	47,176	1,744	-53	687	1,110
1983	47,176	51,865	4,689	2,900	1,912	-123
Total changes			31,206	19,294	8,296	3,616

MEMO		
Total profits	Distributed profits	(8) as % of (7)
(7)	(8)	(9)
5,414	3,040	56.2
3,151	1,903	60.4
4,165	2,101	50.4
4,190	2,409	57.5
3,406	2,349	69.0
8,860	3,230	36.5
7,662	4,231	55.2
7,306	5,083	69.6
6,323	4,582	72.4
9,060	4,819	53.2
59,537	33,747	56.7
1,920	1,541	80.3
2,244	1,602	71.4
2,478	1,887	76.2
2,716	1,913	70.4
3,044	2,204	72.4
4,116	2,795	67.9
3,621	3,113	86.0
3,579	2,966	82.9
3,585	2,898	80.8
5,237	3,325	63.5
32,540	24,244	74.5

transactions. Moreover, the direct investment position increased sharply as a result of addition of retained profits by an accumulated total of nearly Fl. 26 billion. In the ten-year period 1974-1983 considered here, direct investment abroad produced accumulated profits of Fl. 60 billion (Column 7). Of this total, an average of 43 % was retained. Nearly 57 % of total profits was distributed and entered as such in the balance of payments under 'Investment income'. The changes consequent on exchange rate differences and revaluations were substantial, but largely offset each other: the accumulated amounts were –Fl. 11 billion and Fl. 14 billion respectively.

The foreign direct investment position in the Netherlands showed a slightly less sharp growth in relative terms. From 1973 onwards the amount invested more than doubled to nearly Fl. 52 billion. Of this change, nearly two-thirds (Fl. 19.5 billion) was accounted for by direct investment flows. One-quarter of the increase related to retained profits. It is noteworthy that these non-distributed profits make up only a relatively low percentage (25 %) of total profits. Consequently, of total profits of Fl. 32.5 billion, 75 % – or over Fl. 24 billion – was distributed and included as such in the balance of payments.

The difference in profit distribution percentages for inward and outward direct investment may be connected with the greater need for Netherlands enterprises to undertake cross-border expansion (cf. section 4.2).

Comparison of the distributed profit figures from the survey (Column 8) and those from the balance-of-payments cash registration (investment income) shows that these data are generally in fair agreement. This is also true of the capital flow figures from the survey (Column 4) and the direct investment flow figures from the balance-of-payments registration.

Nevertheless, differences may occur since the survey relates to a somewhat more limited group than the balance-of-payments registration. Furthermore, differences may occur from year to year owing to items in transit.

5 Direct investment and rates of return, by sector

The movements in direct investment by and in the various sectors are frequently connected with the developments in the various countries. Viewed from this angle, it would be interesting to include the country aspect from the very start in the discussion of the distribution of direct investment among the various sectors. Yet, to promote clarity of presentation, the sectoral aspects will be outlined first (Chapter 5), followed by the geographical distribution (Chapter 6), after which the cross relations between the two will be analysed (Chapter 7). This does not, of course, exclude that these relations may already crop up earlier.

The breakdown by sector is, in principle, made on the basis of the Netherlands situation (sections 5.1 and 5.2). Thus, direct investment by a Netherlands metal company in a chemical company abroad is shown under the metal industry, and direct investment by a foreign metal company in a Netherlands trading company is recorded under trade. Consequently, for outward direct investment the classification criterion is the Netherlands sector of *origin;* for inward direct investment, it is the Netherlands sector of *destination.* Companies whose operations cover more than one sector have been classed in their entirety on the basis of their principal activity. Moreover, as from 1981, the enterprises included in the survey were asked to state both the sector of origin and the sector of destination for both inward and outward investment. The consequences of an alternative classification are reviewed in section 5.4.

5.1 Netherlands direct investment abroad

5.1.1 Production industries

Between 1973 and 1983 Netherlands direct investment originating from the production industries (including construction and agriculture) more than doubled, from nearly Fl. 40 billion to over Fl. 94 billion (Chart 4 and Appendix E). This means an average annual growth rate of nearly 9.5 % in nominal terms; the growth rate accelerated from 5.5 % per annum in the first half of the period to 13.5 % per annum in the second. In terms of both volume and growth, oil and chemicals held pride of place within total direct investment by the production industries, recording an average annual growth rate of 12 %, speeding up from 3.5 % in the first half of the period to 21 % in the second (Table 5).

In value terms, the metal and electrical engineering industries ranked second. In the period 1973-1983 direct investment by this sector expanded by an annual average

Table 5
Average growth rates of and rates of return on Netherlands direct investment abroad, broken down by sector

Sector	Growth rates			Rates of return		
	1974/ 1978	1979/ 1983	1974/ 1983	1974/ 1978	1979/ 1983	1974/ 1983
Production industries						
– mining and quarrying, oil and chemicals	3.5	20.8	11.8	12.5	14.5	13.5
– metals and electrical engineering	6.6	3.3	5.0	4.2	3.3	3.8
– food, drink and tobacco	6.8	2.6	4.7	8.7	11.7	10.2
– other [1]	14.1	6.3	10.1	4.2	6.5	5.3
Total production industries	5.3	13.3	9.3	9.2	11.0	10.1
Services						
– trade	11.3	17.6	14.4	.	.	.
– transport, storage and communication	2.7	–0.5	1.1	.	.	.
– banking and insurance	18.0	27.9	22.9	.	.	.
– other [2]	28.5	25.5	27.0	.	.	.
Total services	13.8	20.3	17.0	5.2 [3]	5.8 [3]	5.5 [3]
Grand total	6.7	14.6	10.6	8.7	10.1	9.4

[1] Including agriculture and fishing, and construction.
[2] Includes investment companies, real estate companies, mortgage banks, savings banks and commercial services.
[3] For reasons of confidentiality, no specification can be given of the return rates in the services sector.

of 5 %. However, the second half of the period saw a considerable growth deceleration compared with the first: 3.5 % against with 6.5 %.

After 1981, the outstanding amount even showed a substantial decrease in absolute terms, owing to structurally adverse developments in the iron and steel-making industry in particular, which led to a sharp contraction of multinational operations. Direct investment by the food, drink and tobacco industry exhibited an average annual growth rate of 4.5 %, levelling off from 7 % in the first half of the period to 2.5 % in the second.

The share of the production industries in total Netherlands outward direct investment declined from 88 % in 1973 to 78.5 % in 1983. This relative decrease was accounted for by the metal and the food, drink and tobacco industries. On the other hand, the share of oil and chemicals in total outward direct investment went up by 6 percentage points, to 53.5 % (Chart 4).

5.1.2 Services

Quintupling from Fl. 5.5 billion to Fl. 25.5 billion, direct investment abroad by the Netherlands services sector showed a spectacular development between 1973 and 1983. This development meant a very substantial annual growth rate of 17 % in nominal terms; especially the second half of the period saw a sharp growth acceleration, to 20.5 %, compared with 14 % in the first half (Table 5). This growth was underlain by the emergence of Netherlands multinational enterprises in the services sector. Meanwhile, some of these enterprises have grown to such an extent that, in terms of size, they are catching up with the leading group of large Netherlands multinationals in the production industries.

The growth was primarily accounted for by the banking and insurance and pension fund sectors, and centred on the latter half of the period; however, after 1982, some levelling-off was apparent (Chapter 7). For the group 'other services', the rate of growth was even more marked; direct investment by investment and real estate companies in particular showed a sharp upward tendency. The trade sector also saw a sharp increase in its direct investment position abroad (14.5 % per annum), major advances being made by retail trade. On the other hand, direct investment by the transport and storage sector showed barely any growth, even registering, on average, a slight decline in absolute terms in the second half of the period.

The very strong growth of direct investment by the services sector caused the share of services in the total direct investment position abroad to increase from over 12 % in 1973 to 21.5 % in 1983, at the expense of the share of the production industries.

5.1.3 Rates of return and growth

The level of and the movements in the rates of return on Netherlands direct investment abroad by the various sectors showed considerable fluctuations around the overall level of 9.5 % (Table 5).

Oil and chemicals were clearly above this overall average. The food, drink and tobacco industry achieved an average rate of return of over 10 %, whereas the metal industry realized a relatively low rate of less than 4 %. The latter figure was notably depressed by the contraction referred to earlier and by absorption of losses (section 5.1.1). In this context, it might be noted that Stopford and Dunning's study reveals a similar pattern worldwide as regards differences in rates of return among the various sectors of the production industries.[13] At an average of 5.5 %, the rate of return achieved by the services sector as a whole was far below the overall average (Chart 5).

---

[13] Stopford and Dunning, *op. cit.*

The divergent movements in growth and return in the various sectors give rise to the question whether there is a relationship between the rate of growth and the rate of return. It would be obvious to assume that a favourable development of return on a sector's direct investment abroad will stimulate the growth of such investment. To a certain extent this growth ensues automatically insofar as relatively higher levels of retained profit lead to relatively higher direct investment positions. It is evident from Table 5 that the comparatively very favourable rates of return in oil and chemicals have been attended with very high average growth rates. In the metal industry (and iron and steel-making in particular) the low rates of return would distinctly appear to be reflected in the rate of growth, although it must be noted that losses and break-ups of transnational units did, of course, have a depressing effect on both return and growth.

However, there are also examples pointing in the other direction. Thus, the relatively favourable development of return in the food industry was accompanied by a relatively modest growth. However, this may have been due to the fact that, notably in the second half of the period, some very large Netherlands multinationals in the food sector were in a stage of consolidation, pursuing increased earning capacity rather than expansion.

The development of return rates in the services sector, too, was fairly meagre compared with the strong growth in this sector. These relatively modest results were primarily caused by the depressed state of affairs in certain sub-sectors. A case in point was the structurally unfavourable development worldwide in transport and storage. As a result, growth in this area was nil. A role was also played by the fact that it was only in the period covered by this study that the service enterprises undertook large-scale multinationalization. Return rates may have been depressed by the initial cost of investment. In the literature, start-up periods of seven or eight years are sometimes mentioned.[14] In this context, it is significant to note that return in the trade sector – where multinationalization boasts a much longer tradition – did show a relatively satisfactory development.

[14] Cf. De Volkskrant, October 1, 1985.

5.2 Foreign direct investment in the Netherlands

5.2.1 Production industries

Between end-1973 and end-1983, the foreign direct investment position in the Netherlands production industries (including construction and agriculture) doubled from Fl. 15 billion to Fl. 30 billion (Chart 6). This meant an average growth of 7 % per annum, or, 2 percentage points less than the growth of outward direct investment. Contrary to outward direct investment, inward direct investment showed barely any growth acceleration in the second half of the period (Table 6). The growth rate was depressed especially by developments after 1981, when the contractions and break-ups of transnational units in the metal industry referred to earlier left their mark on inward direct investment as well. In the food sector the growth rate admittedly also

Table 6
Average growth rates of and rates of return on foreign direct investment in the Netherlands, broken down by sector

Sector	Growth rates			Rates of return		
	1974/ 1978	1979/ 1983	1974/ 1983	1974/ 1978	1979/ 1983	1974/ 1983
Production industries						
– mining and quarrying, oil and chemicals	4.0	10.3	7.1	15.4	19.2	17.3
– metals and electrical engineering	9.2	1.1	5.1	4.6	6.0	5.3
– food, drink and tobacco	15.0	9.6	12.2	7.2	8.9	8.1
– other [1]	5.7	8.2	7.0	10.5	7.0	8.7
Total production industries	6.6	7.6	7.1	11.5	13.3	12.4
Services						
– trade	13.5	13.4	13.5	.	.	.
– transport, storage and communication	12.5	-2.8	4.6	.	.	.
– banking and insurance	13.2	17.2	15.2	.	.	.
– other [2]	17.5	20.2	18.8	.	.	.
Total services	14.3	15.3	14.8	9.9 [3]	9.7 [3]	9.8 [3]
Grand total	8.8	10.4	9.6	11.1	11.9	11.5

1 Including agriculture and fishing, and construction.
2 Includes investment companies, real estate companies, mortgage banks, savings banks and commercial services.
3 For reasons of confidentiality, no specification can be given of the return rates in the services sector.

decelerated, but still reached a respectable 9.5 % in the second half of the period, considerably more than the growth rate of outward direct investment in this sector. In the period as a whole, direct investment in the Netherlands food industry recorded the highest growth rate (12 %) within the production industries. Consequently, this sector's share in the total direct investment position went up slightly.

As a result of the relatively low growth rates for the other sectors of the production industries, the share of the production industries in the overall amount of foreign direct investment fell very markedly, from 74 % to 58 %.

5.2.2 *Services*

Growing at an average of 15 %, foreign direct investment in the Netherlands services sector developed less exuberantly than this sector's outward direct investment. Yet, this growth rate was more than twice that recorded for inward direct investment in the production industries. The trade sector showed an average growth rate of 13.5 %, banking and insurance 15 % and other services 19 %. The growth rate of direct investment in the transport, storage and communication sector was again depressed (5 %), and likewise showed a decline in absolute terms in the second half of the period. This sector apart, the relatively rapid growth in the remaining sectors of services caused the share of services in total inward direct investment to increase from 26 % to 42 %.

5.2.3 *Rates of return and growth*

Viewed over time and by sector, the return rates on foreign direct investment in the Netherlands also showed wide fluctuations around the overall average of 11.5 % (Table 6 and Chart 7). Like outward direct investment, inward direct investment yielded the highest average return rate in oil and chemicals (17.5 %). The return rates in the food industry and in the other production industries averaged 8-9 %. Return rates on inward direct investment in the metal industry, however, were also at a low average level (5.5 %), although towards the end of the period a recovery would appear to have set in. The return rate on inward direct investment in services averaged 10 %. Again, the return rates in transport and storage were far below, and those in the other sectors above, this average. As this foreign direct investment is generally of an earlier date and more 'mature' than that of the Netherlands services sector abroad, the depressing effect of initial losses, etc. presumably played a smaller role than in the case of outward direct investment in this sector. Again, as shown in Table 6, there would generally appear to be a relationship between the rates of return on and the growth rates of direct investment: high return rates were generally attended by high growth rates. An exception was oil and chemicals, where the growth rate, especially in the first half of the period, was meagre compared with the high rates of return. It may be presumed that the structural overcapacity in this sector after the first oil crisis played a role in this respect (Chapter 7). In the metal industry, low return rates were again attended by low growth rates.

5.3 Net direct investment position

As is shown in Chart 8, the net direct investment position of the *production industries* was positive in that outward direct investment exceeded inward direct investment throughout (Dunning's terminology). The surplus tripled from over Fl. 20 billion in 1973 to nearly Fl. 65 billion in 1983. Apparently, the Netherlands production industries have long established themselves ever more firmly in a highly developed stage, presumably attended by increasing specialization and exploitation of specific regional advantages.

The development of the net position of *services* suggests that, in the period 1973-1983, this sector moved from somewhere between Dunning's second and third stages to the fourth. Phrased differently: whereas until the 1980s inward direct investment exceeded outward direct investment in this sector, it has been increasingly clear that the tables have been turned since 1980. This turnround notably related to banking and insurance and to the other financial services sector. Apparently, here too, the urge or the need to come to expansion across the national borders has been translated into action, opening up new possibilities for product specialization, etc.

5.4 Sector of origin and sector of destination

When undertaking direct investment abroad, an enterprise from a certain Netherlands sector need not necessarily participate in an enterprise forming part of the same sector. To enable an assessment of the magnitude of the differences in direct investment classification on different criteria, the questionnaire used in the surveys on outward direct investment – which is traditionally classified by sector of origin – was extended, from 1981 onwards, by the inclusion of a question about the sector of destination of this investment. Likewise, the reporting form for inward direct investment, which is traditionally classified by sector of destination (in the Netherlands), was extended by the inclusion of a question about the foreign sector of origin. The results and the differences for 1983 are summarized in Table 7.

The Table shows that outward direct investment by the production industries broadly finds its way to the same sectors. The *total* difference is merely Fl. 0.5 billion. Apparently, this sector generally sticks to its last. In the services sector, the differences are larger, especially in trade and in other services.

The classification differences indicate that the Netherlands trade sector in particular undertakes direct investment in other services, suggesting allied operations. The group of Netherlands private individuals also invests in other services, but the significance of this investment is limited.

For inward direct investment, the classification differences for the production industries prove to be relatively larger. The differences in oil and chemicals are admittedly very minor, but the figures show that direct investment in the Netherlands by foreign enterprises from the metal industry is not always in the Netherlands metal industry. These foreign enterprises invest notably in the Netherlands trade sector, presumably to set up trading establishments, etc.

Table 7
Differences between sector of origin and sector of destination, 1983
(billions of guilders)

Sector	Capital participation, outward			Capital participation, inward		
	Origin	Destination	Difference	Origin	Destination	Difference
Agriculture and fishing	–	0.1	0.1	0.1	0.1	–
Production industries						
– mining and quarrying, oil and chemicals	57.2	56.1	-1.1	11.1	11.8	0.7
– metals and electrical engineering	15.3	15.9	0.6	4.7	6.6	1.9
– food, drink and tobacco	7.6	7.2	-0.4	3.1	3.6	0.5
– other	1.1	1.5	0.4	1.8	1.8	–
Total production industries	81.2	80.7	-0.5	20.7	23.8	3.1
Construction	0.8	0.6	-0.2	0.1	0.1	–
Services						
– trade	6.2	4.1	-2.1	6.9	2.8	-4.1
– transport, storage and communication	1.1	1.0	-0.1	0.3	0.2	-0.1
– banking and insurance	6.3	6.2	-0.1	4.5	4.7	0.2
– other	4.9	8.3	3.4	4.3	4.7	0.4
Total services	18.5	19.6	1.1	16.0	12.4	-3.6
Private individuals	0.5	–	-0.5	–	0.5	0.5
Grand total	101.0	101.0	–	36.9	36.9	–

6 Direct investment and rates of return, by country

The analysis of direct investment by country, presented in this Chapter, generally focuses on *groups* of countries. This is done for reasons of perspicuity as well as confidentiality, since a specification by country might in some cases reveal undue details about the direct investment positions of individual reporting enterprises. The breakdown used thus far distinguished between the EC countries (excluding Greece, Spain and Portugal), Switzerland, the United States, the other developed countries and the developing countries in each of the continents (the Netherlands Antilles being shown separately). Thanks to the cooperation of the reporting enterprises, it is now also possible, for the figures from 1981 onwards, to distinguish, within the total group of developing countries, the groups of newly industrializing countries (NICs), low-income countries and target countries; target countries are those countries on which Netherlands development aid was concentrated in the period covered.

6.1 Netherlands direct investment abroad

6.1.1 EC

Between 1973 and 1983, Netherlands direct investment in the EC more than doubled, from Fl. 22.5 billion to Fl. 46.5 billion (see e.g. Chart 9). This means an average annual growth rate of 7.5 %. The figures for the various countries and the various years showed wide fluctuations around this average. For instance, direct investment in the Federal Republic of Germany decreased in nominal terms in the second half of the period, while the growth of direct investment in France was also depressed; the break-ups of units and the contraction in the metal industry, referred to earlier, played a role in this respect. On the other hand, the growth rate of direct investment in the United Kingdom increased sharply, owing to such factors as North Sea oil and gas exploration; direct investment in the other EC countries (Ireland and Denmark) also benefitted from this development and showed a distinct acceleration (see also Table 10).

In the period covered by this study, the share of direct investment in the EC in total outward direct investment fell from nearly 51 % to barely 39 %. This decrease was wholly accounted for by the Federal Republic of Germany, France, and Belgium and Luxembourg. The shares of the United Kingdom and of Ireland and Denmark, on the other hand, increased slightly.

6.1.2 *United States*

In the period concerned, Netherlands direct investment in the United States more than quintupled, from Fl. 6 billion in 1973 to Fl. 33.5 billion in 1983. This means an average annual growth rate of 18.5 %, nearly two-and-a-half times the growth rate of direct investment in the EC. Notably the late 1970s saw a marked growth acceleration: an average of 25.5 % against 11.5 % in the first half of the period. This strong growth caused the share of the United States in total Netherlands outward direct investment to double to nearly 30 %.

To explain the attraction of the United States as a direct investment destination, compared notably with the EC, various reasons are advanced:

- The United States is the world's largest *homogeneous* market. Within this market, there is a large and varied demand for high-quality products and services. Consequently, in principle, the growth opportunities are large and widely spread.
- In the United States, science and technology are very highly advanced, with various centres of competence; this is a most important factor. Additionally, US society in general may be rated as innovation-conscious. This means that, for many enterprises, a presence in the United States is a prerequisite for access to new know-how.
- The political stability of the country is a major factor for enterprises which take a long-term view in their investment decisions.
- The societal and economic freedom guarantees that foreign investors have free access and ensures that they can operate on an equal footing with domestic producers.[15]
- Cost increases relative to other countries have been fairly small. For instance, in the period 1965-1975 average wages in the production industries went up by 80 % in the United States, 109 % in Canada, 150 % in the Federal Republic of Germany, 207 % in the United Kingdom and 307 % in Japan.[16] In other areas as well – such as taxes – costs for enterprises are most probably lower in the United States than they are elsewhere.

  The advantages in terms of relative costs would also appear to be reflected in the relatively high rates of return on Netherlands direct investment in the United States (section 6.1.5).
- The decrease in the dollar's exchange rate in the 1970s provided foreign enterprises with a strong incentive to expand their direct investment in the United States, as the price of such investment expressed in their own currencies was decreasing, making acquisitions cheaper. For the Netherlands, a case in point is

---

[15] Also see, for instance: *Results of a survey of Dutch investors that have established operations in the United States,* The Netherlands Chamber of Commerce in the United States, 1983.

[16] The Economist, *Business Brief,* May 21, 1983, pp. 98-99.

the previously mainly guilder-based enterprises in the services sector. Especially in the second half of the period covered, these enterprises strongly expanded their holdings in the United States, although in recent years – when the dollar recovered – some redress has been apparent (Chapter 7).[17]

Stopford and Dunning's study of the development of investment by multinational enterprises shows that the pull exerted by the United States on foreign direct investors was not limited to Netherlands enterprises, but extended to those from other European countries as well.[18] These authors note that, since the mid-1970s, these enterprises have become ever more aware of the increasing saturation of the traditional European markets and the relatively imperfect functioning of these markets, while profitability in Europe has been less than adequate, as is also reflected in the comparatively very low return on Netherlands direct investment in other European countries (section 6.1.5). Even though this increasing orientation towards the United States and turning-away from Europe ensued from these comparatively stagnating factors, they in turn had the effect of intensifying the slowdown of growth in Europe, giving rise to a downward spiralling motion. Illustrative of this effect is the relative decline of EC direct investment in the Netherlands (section 6.2.1).

6.1.3 Other developed countries

Of total Netherlands direct investment in the group of other developed countries, that in Switzerland deserves special mention. It increased from Fl. 1 billion at end-1973 to Fl. 5.5 billion at end-1983, implying an average growth rate of over 18 % per annum. This growth was notably accounted for by the metal and food industries and by almost all sectors of services. The levelling-off of the growth rate in the second half of the period caused the relative share of Switzerland, which had initially mounted sharply, to decline slightly in the late 1970s, coming out at 4.5 % in 1983.

6.1.4 Developing countries

The movements in Netherlands direct investment in the developing countries showed considerable divergencies. Thus, in the first half of the period the growth of Netherlands direct investment in this group of countries was wholly accounted for by the developing countries in Africa. This was, however, largely due to direct investment by the oil and chemical industries, which showed a very forceful expansion in some countries of this continent after the first oil crisis. Since this investment distorts

---

[17] Cf. A.H.E.M. Wellink, *Netherlands exporters and international competition*, De Nederlandsche Bank N.V., Quarterly Bulletin 1985/1.

[18] Stopford and Dunning, *op. cit.*

the overall pattern of direct investment in the developing countries, Table 8 also shows the growth rates exclusive of oil and chemicals.

The growth pattern excluding oil and chemicals reveals that – the Netherlands Antilles apart – it was notably direct investment in the developing countries of Asia which developed very favourably, growing at an average of 12 % per annum (9 % in the first half of the period and over 15 % in the second). The share of Asia in total Netherlands outward direct investment thus rose to above 5 %. One factor in this regard has undoubtedly been the relatively very high rates of return on Netherlands direct investment in the countries of Asia (section 6.1.5).

In this context, the question may be raised to what extent it should be expected that direct investment will play a more important role in the flow of external finance to developing countries with balance-of-payments problems, whether 'spontaneously' or depending upon prospects of growth and profitability. In a speech held at the annual meeting of the Netherlands Finance Company for Developing Countries, H.R.H. Prince Claus pointed out the major contribution which direct investment may make in helping developing countries cope with the difficult position in which many of them find themselves in the present adverse world economic climate [19]: 'Direct investment may be regarded as a tangible and valuable *trait d'union* between industrialized and developing countries. First, it is a form of financing which does not create direct external indebtedness, as borrowing does; it is a form of direct cooperation. An added advantage is that the business risks are shared by residents of the host country and the foreign direct investors. Another factor which is of major importance in this respect is the role of direct investment in the transfer of knowledge, technological know-how and management skills. This industrial transfer of know-how, notably to the least developed countries, enables something to be transferred which is indispensable for any form of industrialization: the art of the entrepreneur. Capital with value added'.

The World Bank also recognizes direct investment's importance to developing countries. Under its auspices, the Multilateral Investment Guarantee Agency (MIGA), whose aim is to increase the flow of investment funds to the developing countries, was set up recently. The MIGA offers investing enterprises insurance against non-commercial risks, such as war and nationalization. Additionally, the International Finance Corporation, a subsidiary of the World Bank set up in 1956, is increasingly active in assisting enterprises in investing in the Third World.

Actual developments with regard to Netherlands direct investment in the developing countries (excluding the Netherlands Antilles) in the period 1973-1983 resulted in a decrease in these countries' share in total outward direct investment,

[19] H.R.H. Prince Claus, *Speech at the Annual Meeting of the Finance Company for Developing Countries*, The Hague, May 2, 1985.

Table 8
Average growth rates of Netherlands direct investment in developing countries

Country/group of countries	Total			Ditto, excluding oil and chemicals		
	1974/ 1978	1979/ 1983	1974/ 1983	1974/ 1978	1979/ 1983	1974/ 1983
Developing countries						
– Europe	2.4	3.2	2.8	6.0	3.8	4.9
– Africa	34.0	14.1	23.7	5.1	-3.2	0.9
– Asia	4.6	23.1	13.5	8.8	15.3	12.0
– Latin America (excluding Netherlands Antilles)	1.6	8.7	5.1	6.8	5.7	6.2
– Netherlands Antilles	11.4	9.6	10.5	19.1	9.9	14.4
Total developing countries	6.9	12.2	9.5	11.3	8.3	9.8

from 13.5 % in 1973 to 11.5 % in 1983 (Chart 9). This relative decline was accounted for by the developing countries in Latin America and Europe. Moreover, for the developing countries in Africa, the growth rates were relatively low, notably outside the oil and chemical industries (Chart 8). The patterns are revealed even more clearly by a breakdown of the developing countries by development stage: the NICs, the low-income countries and the so-called target countries. Table 9 shows the positions for the period 1981-1983.

It is noteworthy that, in two years' time, the position in the NICs nearly doubled to Fl. 6 billion. The share of these countries in total direct investment in the developing countries considered thus increased from 31 % to 43 %, at the expense of investment in, for instance, the low-income countries, whether target countries or not. On the other hand, the share of the other target countries rose to 4.5 %. Considering the composition of this group of countries (Egypt, Zambia, Colombia, Yemen), it may be possible that these countries, too, have passed the minimum (first) stage of development, so that increasingly favourable conditions are being created for foreign establishments and investment.

The pattern of Netherlands direct investment in the developing countries is in line with that established in other studies, dealing with worldwide direct investment. Stopford and Dunning's study, for example, shows that the share of the developing countries in worldwide inward direct investment decreased from 32 % in 1960 to 31 % in 1971 and 27 % in 1980.[20]

---

[20] Stopford and Dunning, *op. cit.*, pp. 11 ff.

Table 9
Netherlands direct investment position in some groups of developing countries (end-of-year figures)

Group of countries	1981		1982		1983	
	millions of guilders	% of total developing countries [1]	millions of guilders	% of total developing countries [1]	millions of guilders	% of total developing countries [1]
Newly industrializing countries [2]	3,551	31.1	5,305	42.4	6,003	43.2
Low-income countries which are also target countries [3]	1,227	10.7	680	5.5	687	4.9
Other low-income countries	315	2.8	201	1.6	226	1.6
Other target countries [4]	207	1.8	403	3.2	608	4.4
Middle East	614	5.4	895	7.2	813	5.9
Total	5,914	51.8	7,484	59.9	8,337	60.0

[1] Excluding Netherlands Antilles.
[2] Mexico, Brazil, Argentina, Singapore, South Korea, Taiwan, Hong Kong.
[3] Sudan, Upper Volta, Kenya, Tanzania, Pakistan, India, Sri Lanka, Bangladesh, Indonesia.
[4] Egypt, Zambia, Colombia, Yemen.

This study also shows that it was notably the NICs which accounted for the lion's share of the growth of direct investment in the developing countries. The authors list the following factors as the principal causes underlying this growth: investment-friendly, measures and facilities for foreign investors, cheap and skilled labour, and large domestic markets with relatively rich consumers.

H.R.H. Prince Claus, too, noted in his speech that the bulk of foreign direct investment in the developing countries was accounted for by the NICs and the Mature Industrialized Countries (MICs): '... in 1981, 44 % and 27 % respectively. The poorest countries, the Less Developed Countries (LDCs), succeeded in attracting no more than 4 %. Their position has worsened in relative terms; five years earlier, they had still succeeded in attracting 8 % of the total flow'.

Furthermore, a recent IMF study also points out the unequal distribution of direct investment among the developing countries.[21] Finally, an investigation conducted by the Group of Thirty, in which 52 internationally operating enterprises were inter-

[21] IMF Occasional Paper, no. 33, *Foreign Private Investment in Developing Countries*, by David Goldsbrough, IMF, 1985.

viewed about their international investment plans, showed that in the period 1983-1987 these enterprises will direct their investment activity primarily towards NICs in Southeast Asia.[22]

6.1.5 Rates of return and growth

A breakdown of rates of growth and return by country and group of countries again broadly shows the relationship between the rate of return on and the rate of growth of direct investment. Thus, the relatively low rates of return in the EC were attended by an, on average, relatively low growth rate (Table 10 and Chart 10). The twice-as-high average return in the group of other developed countries (12.5 %) was accompanied by an, on average, twice-as-high growth rate of direct investment (14.5 %). For the group of developing countries, too, both the rates of return and the average growth rates were higher than for the EC. Especially the rates of return achieved in the developing countries of Asia were strikingly high, averaging nearly 20 % and in 1979-1983 even 23 %. Apparently, high rates of return are not merely a prerequisite for direct investment in a country, they are also a condition for a satisfactory growth of such investment.

The question could be raised to what extent such factors as exchange rate fluctuations, differences in tax regulations, differences in investment incentives, differences in invoicing and in balance-sheet valuation have influenced the major differences in return rates between the various countries. The data compiled by means of the surveys do not permit any conclusions in this regard. However, the differences between the continents are apparent throughout the period covered and for practically all sectors, so that they would not seem the result of fortuitous or non-recurring isolated factors. It might furthermore be noted that this pattern of rates of return and growth is also evident from Stopford and Dunning's study and from an investigation made by the EC. Stopford and Dunning give data about the sales of 195 multinational enterprises based in Europe and/or North America.[23] Between 1977 and 1981 the European-based companies in particular reduced the European share in total foreign sales, whereas the North American share increased. Furthermore, the study shows that, between 1977 and 1981, the profitability of the European multinational enterprises declined and that it was less than half that achieved by their Japanese and US-based counterparts. A study conducted by the EC also shows the difference in the 1970s (contrary to the 1960s) in return on investment achieved in the EC and the United States.[24] This subject will be discussed in more detail in the section dealing with return rates on foreign direct investment in the Netherlands (section 6.2.5).

---

22 Group of Thirty, *Foreign direct investment 1973-1987,* New York, 1984, pp. 23 ff.

23 Stopford and Dunning, *op. cit.*

24 J. Mortensen, *Rentabiliteit, relatieve factorprijzen en substitutie kapitaal/arbeid in de Gemeenschap, de Verenigde Staten en Japan – 1960/1983,* Europese Economie, July 1984.

Table 10
Average growth rates of and rates of return on Netherlands direct investment abroad, broken down by country

Country/group of countries	Growth rates			Rates of return		
	1974/ 1978	1979/ 1983	1974/ 1983	1974/ 1978	1979/ 1983	1974/ 1983
EC						
– Belgium and Luxembourg	8.1	10.0	9.1	1.6	4.5	3.1
– Federal Republic of Germany	2.5	-2.4	0.0	3.2	2.1	2.6
– France	8.2	2.7	5.4	8.5	-2.0	3.3
– United Kingdom	5.6	18.7	12.0	7.7	12.6	10.1
– Other EC countries, excluding Greece	3.7	24.8	13.7	5.0	17.2	11.1
Total EC	5.1	10.0	7.6	5.3	7.5	6.4
Other developed countries						
– United States	11.7	25.4	18.3	12.7	11.4	12.0
– Switzerland	26.9	10.1	18.2	14.3	15.1	14.7
– Other [1]	-0.7	18.5	8.5	11.5	11.6	11.5
Total other developed countries	8.4	21.3	14.7	12.7	12.0	12.3
Total developing countries	6.9	12.2	9.5	10.7	12.8	11.7
Grand total	6.7	14.6	10.6	8.7	10.1	9.4

[1] For reasons of confidentiality, no separate figures can be given for Japan.

6.2 Foreign direct investment in the Netherlands

6.2.1 EC

Direct investment in the Netherlands by European enterprises nearly doubled between 1973 and 1983, from Fl. 9 billion to Fl. 16.5 billion. The growth rate thus averaged 6.5 % per annum; the growth was notably achieved in the second half of the period, when the expansion of direct investment from practically all EC countries showed an acceleration. A notable exception was direct investment from the Federal Republic of Germany, which increased hardly. Thus, Germany only barely succeeded in maintaining its position as the second largest European investor in the Netherlands, behind the United Kingdom.

Viewed for the period as a whole, however, the growth of European direct investment in the Netherlands was distinctly lower than that of direct investment from other (groups of) countries. As a result, the EC had to yield its position as the largest foreign direct investor in the Netherlands to the United States. As is shown in Chart 11, the share of the EC in total inward direct investment fell by more than 10 percentage points, from 43 % in 1973 to 31.5 % in 1983. This fall was notably due to a relative decrease in direct investment in the production industries (section 7.1.2).

The overview of the number and the countries of origin of foreign enterprises' establishments in the Netherlands, presented in Chart 12 – derived from the survey as at January 1, 1984, conducted by the University of Utrecht – shows that until 1946 pride of place was held by establishments of enterprises from *Europe* (notably the United Kingdom). After the Second World War, the share of Europe declined, initially in favour of the number of establishments from the United States and later those from Japan. Within Europe, the Federal Republic of Germany accounted for a relatively considerable share in the number of establishments in the post-war period until 1975. That period witnessed a wave of direct investment by mainly German and US enterprises in our 'Golden Delta', centring on the production industries (especially the metal and chemical industries). It was these very sectors which had to cope with structural problems in the 1970s.

With regard to the establishments set up later in the most recent period 1975-1984, the share of the Federal Republic of Germany showed a consequent decrease, in favour of such countries as the United Kingdom, Japan and Switzerland. In this respect, a role was played by the shift in direct investment away from the production industries and towards services (section 7.1.2).

The shift in European (industrial) investors' preferences away from the Netherlands and those of Netherlands (industrial) investors away from Europe is not an isolated phenomenon; this is evident from comparable data on direct investment for the Federal Republic of Germany, France and the United Kingdom, which also indicate a preference for other continents, notably the United States and Asia (section 6.2.5).

6.2.2 United States

In the period 1973-1983 direct investment from the United States increased by an average of 9 % per annum to Fl. 18 billion. The United States thus remained the largest individual direct investor in the Netherlands. However, the US share in inward direct investment showed a slight decline, from 37 % in 1973 to nearly 35 % in 1983.

Viewed in the somewhat longer term, US direct investment in the Netherlands began to increase in the late 1950s, and reached a high in the 1960s, followed by a relative decline (see also Chart 1). Notably the second half of the 1970s saw the direct investment surge slow down or even come to an end, particularly in the production industries. This is also illustrated by Chart 12, which shows the number of foreign enterprises' establishments set up in the Netherlands. In the period 1946-1959 the US share in the total number of new establishments of foreign enterprises reached its highest level – albeit that the absolute number of new establishments was still fairly small. In the years 1960-1974 this number increased very sharply, with the US share declining slightly. Subsequently, this share decreased further, while the absolute number of new establishments fell sharply.

These fluctuations in US direct investors' preference for the Netherlands (and the rest of Europe) were probably due in large measure to location factors, such as economic growth, labour costs and the availability of labour. Thus, the strong growth of US direct investment in the Netherlands (and the rest of Europe) in the 1950s and 1960s may be attributed notably to the expansion of the European market, the relatively low unit costs and the adequate supply of skilled labour. In the 1970s, however, most of these advantages were reversed. First, unit costs in Europe had increased sharply in the course of time. Subsequently, this development was accentuated by a decrease in the dollar's exchange rate, which naturally had the effect of raising the dollar price of potential acquisitions in Europe. Additionally, economic growth was slowing down. The combination of higher costs and lower economic growth depressed profitability, much more so than in the United States. This not only meant that Europe was losing much of its attraction for US direct investors, it also caused Netherlands and other European entrepreneurs to orient their international direct investment activity increasingly towards the United States. A discussion of the prospects for US (and other) direct investment in the Netherlands is given in Chapter 7.

6.2.3 Other developed countries

In addition to the United States, Switzerland was another major direct investor within the group of developed countries outside the EC. Swiss direct investment in the Netherlands increased from Fl. 2 billion in 1973 to over Fl. 5.5 billion in 1983 – an average growth rate of 11 % per annum. Thus, Switzerland has become the fourth largest direct investor in the Netherlands, behind the United States, the United Kingdom and the Netherlands Antilles. The share of Switzerland in total inward direct investment increased slightly, from 10 % in 1973 to 11 % in 1983.

Averaging 14 % per annum, the growth of direct investment in the Netherlands from the other developed countries distinctly exceeded the overall average. This investment more than tripled, from Fl. 1 billion at end-1973 to Fl. 3.5 billion in 1983. Within this group, Japan holds pride of place. Direct investment from Japan increased nearly tenfold to close on Fl. 1.5 billion in 1983. Japan's share increased to

2.5 %, from 0.8 % in 1973. The survey conducted by the University of Utrecht also shows a sharp increase in the number of new establishments of Japanese enterprises, especially in recent years (Chart 12). This development may have been due notably to the increasing internationalization of Japanese enterprises in the 1970s and the 1980s. It might be noted here that at present only 3 % of total Japanese corporate output is accounted for by establishments outside Japan. In this connection, a Japanese study group has recommended, in a report to the Japanese Ministry of Trade and Industry (MITI), that direct investment abroad should be encouraged.[25] In 1984 Japan invested $ 1.9 billion (1983: $ 1 billion) in Western Europe, which thus dislodged Asia from the third position on the list of Japan's direct investment destinations.

In 1983, the direct investment position of the rest of the group of other developed countries was Fl. 2 billion, against over Fl. 0.5 billion in 1973.

6.2.4 *Developing countries*

In the period considered, direct investment from the developing countries increased from Fl. 1 billion to Fl. 8.5 billion. This increase occurred across the board, with the exception of the developing countries in Africa. The largest single direct investor was the Netherlands Antilles, but such investment cannot really be regarded as having its origin in that country itself as it emanates to a major extent from Netherlands companies which have moved their registered office to the Antilles.

A noteworthy feature was the growth of direct investment from the developing countries of Asia, which accelerated in the second half of the period. These countries' share in total inward direct investment increased to nearly 2 %. Apparently these countries are progressing towards the development stage where the national industries have sufficient strength and know-how for cross-border operations in the form of direct investment. Direct investment from Latin America, even if the Netherlands Antilles is excluded, showed a growth considerably in excess of the overall average, but this growth was largely due to the development of direct investment from Bermuda, the Virgin Islands and Panama.

The development stages which some developing countries are passing through are to a certain extent also reflected in Netherlands inward direct investment, especially so if the various groups of developing countries are distinguished, such as NICs, low-income countries, etc. As is evident from Table 11, direct investment from the NICs and from certain target countries (notably in Asia) was significant, whereas that from the other low-income and the other target countries remained nil. The growth of direct investment from the Middle East shows that the oil-producing countries increasingly undertake investment in our country as well.

---

[25] Het Financieele Dagblad, August 21, 1985.

Table 11
Direct investment positions of some groups of developing countries in the Netherlands (end-of-year figures)

Group of countries	1981		1982		1983	
	millions of guilders	% of total developing countries [1]	millions of guilders	% of total developing countries [1]	millions of guilders	% of total developing countries [1]
Newly industrializing countries [2]	76	4.6	106	5.7	150	6.8
Low-income countries which are also target countries [3]	115	6.9	132	7.0	219	9.9
Other low-income countries	6	0.4	5	0.3	3	–
Other target countries [4]	–	–	–	–	–	–
Middle East	32	1.9	68	3.6	480	21.6
Total	229	13.8	311	16.6	852	38.3

1 Excluding Netherlands Antilles.
2 Mexico, Brazil, Argentina, Singapore, South Korea, Taiwan, Hong Kong.
3 Sudan, Upper Volta, Kenya, Tanzania, Pakistan, India, Sri Lanka, Bangladesh, Indonesia.
4 Egypt, Zambia, Colombia, Yemen.

6.2.5 *Rates of return and growth*

Except for France in the second half of the period, the rates of return on direct investment in the Netherlands by the EC multinationals were very modest in relative terms, averaging less than 6 % (Table 12). Apparently, it is not solely the Netherlands multinational enterprises which achieve no more than a low return on their direct investment in the EC, conversely, the Netherlands is no exception to the rule that the EC multinationals achieve a relatively low return in the EC countries, with all its consequences for the (potential) growth of such direct investment. In the foregoing, the relative decline not only of Netherlands direct investment in the EC but also of EC direct investment in the Netherlands was already pointed out. This would suggest that EC direct investment is being reallocated to other continents, a reallocation which is also evident from similar data with regard to the United Kingdom, the Federal Republic of Germany and France.[26] This shift in European direct investment

26 For instance, the share of the United States in UK outward direct investment also doubled (wholly at the expense of the EC). In the Federal Republic of Germany and France, similar shifts were apparent, albeit that these shifts were less at the expense of the EC than in the United Kingdom and the Netherlands.

Table 12
Average growth rates of and rates of return on foreign direct investment in the Netherlands, broken down by country

Country/group of countries	Growth rates			Rates of return		
	1974/ 1978	1979/ 1983	1974/ 1983	1974/ 1978	1979/ 1983	1974/ 1983
EC						
- Belgium and Luxembourg	3.9	7.2	5.6	8.3	6.0	7.2
- Federal Republic of Germany	1.6	0.4	1.0	0.8	4.1	2.5
- France	7.6	12.1	9.8	4.4	19.1	11.8
- United Kingdom	3.1	13.1	8.0	6.1	6.3	6.2
- Other EC countries, excluding Greece	4.3	32.6	17.6	5.7	3.2	4.4
Total EC	3.3	9.4	6.3	4.8	6.8	5.8
Other developed countries						
- United States	8.4	9.4	8.9	18.4	19.9	19.2
- Switzerland	14.9	6.7	10.8	12.3	7.6	9.9
- Japan	25.7	21.0	23.3	-1.6	4.2	1.3
- Other	14.0	7.8	10.9	11.5	10.9	11.2
Total other developed countries	10.5	9.1	9.8	16.4	16.2	16.3
Total developing countries	24.9	18.5	21.6	9.5	9.8	9.7
Grand total	8.8	10.4	9.6	11.1	11.9	11.5

away from the home market, of course, has in its turn a dampening effect on intra-Community growth. More generally, Stopford and Dunning's study, already referred to, shows that the profitability of the European multinationals decreased between 1977 and 1981 and is less than half that achieved by multinational enterprises based in, for instance, the United States and Japan.[27] In conjunction with these results, the relatively low profitability of Netherlands enterprises in the European market and of European enterprises in the Netherlands market, established on the basis of our data, may give rise to the conclusion that the relatively low profitability of these European multinationals is related to a relatively low profitability in the European market.

Compared with the performance of the European multinationals in the Netherlands market, that of the US-based multinationals is striking. The latter enterprises

[27] Stopford and Dunning, *op. cit.*, pp. 82 ff.

prove to have achieved very high rates of return on their direct investment in the Netherlands. The rates of return on this US direct investment averaged as much as over 19 %, showing little fluctuation during the period considered (see also Chart 13). Moreover, these high rates of return compared with those on direct investment from the EC countries are apparent for all sectors, throwing the differences between US and EC direct investment into even more prominent relief.

One explanatory factor could be the much stricter demands in this respect which the multinationals from the United States make – and are able to make – compared to their European counterparts. It is reported that in practice 'threshold values' of, for instance, 17 % are used. In the event of return rates being considered unsatisfactory, the US enterprises are presumably more inclined and able to dispose of subsidiaries, or to implement cost-cutting programmes, than are the European enterprises, which are traditionally firmly rooted in their domestic and neighbouring markets. In this respect, Andriessen may be quoted, who notes that the United States is such a large country and represents such a vast market that 'the international part of an American enterprise is not seldom somewhat loosely appended. In the majority of cases it forms part of a separate division, the international division, but that division is yet in reality dominated by the Americans in the mother country, so that the true characteristics of the multinational are lost. The centre remains in America and, in terms of its power structure, the enterprise remains largely inward-looking. This does not mean that there are no American international enterprises; there are a fair number of them. But their nature is different from that of a truly multinational enterprise'.[28]

An added factor is that, as shown by research by Professor Ellsworth of the Claremont Graduate School in the United States, US entrepreneurs assign a higher priority to keeping shareholders satisfied than do, for instance, Japanese and European managers, who tend to focus on growth market leadership and ubiquity in major sales markets.[29] Ellsworth notes that the corporate objective most prominent in the minds of US managers is 'the duty to maximize shareholders' wealth'. However, he does sound a warning against the danger that this priority might impair long-term objectives, such as competitive power and long-term growth. According to Ellsworth this is so not only because entrepreneurs in such countries as Japan and the Federal Republic of Germany are able to attract cheaper investment funds, as they (need to) reward their shareholders less generously, but also because, compared with US enterprises, these competitors have often financed a larger part of their operations from relatively

28 Andriessen, *op. cit.*

29 Cf. Richard R. Ellsworth, *Capital markets and competitive decline,* Harvard Business Review, September-October 1985; see also Business Week, August 20, 1985. Compare also R. Buck, who notes that, when considering establishment abroad, US enterprises assign a much greater weight to expected profits than do enterprises from other countries; *Nieuwe Japanse en Amerikaanse industriële vestigingen in West-Europa,* Nijmegen, July 1985; see also NRC, October 30, 1985.

cheap borrowed funds. In Ellsworth's view, unduly high demands as to short-term return on shareholders' equity elsewhere could involve a danger of erosion of the strategic base in the long run.

Another aspect of the – by its very nature – vast and homogeneous home market in the United States is that it might traditionally have generated high profits, to which US enterprises may have become accustomed. Under such conditions, 'returning to home base' in the event of setbacks may become an obvious alternative. Finally, such a home market enables the multinationals to test new products rapidly and on a large scale: the home market as a 'launching pad'. Subsequent introduction in faraway foreign markets will thus be simpler and less costly than for the European multinationals, which must operate in fragmented home markets and progress much less rapidly and much less far on the 'learning curve'.[30]

The rates of return on direct investment from Switzerland and the other developed countries were also above the EC average, albeit less so than those on investment from the United States. Return on direct investment from Japan was still very low in relative terms, but this was probably due to initial costs and initial losses: in 1983 return had already increased to nearly 10%.

The rates of return on direct investment from the developing countries were to a considerable extent determined by those on investment from the Netherlands Antilles. Notably after 1980, these rates fell sharply, especially in transport and storage, trade and other services.

6.3 Net direct investment position

Also when broken down by country and/or group of countries, the Netherlands net foreign direct investment position shows almost invariably surpluses (cf. Chart 14). However, the surplus vis-à-vis the EC countries showed a near-stabilization after 1980, as a result of a stabilization of the position vis-à-vis the United Kingdom, a decrease in the position vis-à-vis the Federal Republic of Germany and France and a slight increase in the position vis-à-vis Belgium and Luxembourg and the group of other EC countries.

Within the group of other developed countries, it is notably the development of the net position vis-à-vis the United States which attracts notice: from a net inward position in 1973 to a distinctly net outward position in 1983. Also with regard to Switzerland, the net inward position declined – to near-equilibrium in 1983.

The net position vis-à-vis the developing countries (excluding the Netherlands Antilles) increased gradually, whereas that vis-à-vis the Netherlands Antilles decreased sharply.

---

[30] Cf. W. Dekker, *High-tech and the changing shape of world trade,* World Trade Conference, Amsterdam, September 5, 1985.

7 Direct investment, by sector and by country

7.1 Structure

7.1.1 Netherlands direct investment abroad

Netherlands direct investment abroad is strongly dominated by the multinational enterprises from the production industries. Notably *oil and chemicals* are of major significance and, during the period considered, these sectors even strengthened their direct investment position further: in 1983 their share in total Netherlands outward direct investment was 53 %, compared with 47 % in 1973 (Table 13 and Chart 15). It is, consequently, no coincidence that these sectors accounted for the largest invested amount per sector/country as represented by their direct investment position in the United States, which in 1983 amounted to 16 % of total Netherlands direct investment abroad (Chart 15). This share, which had still been 10 % in 1973, meant that the United States dislodged the United Kingdom from the first position (Table 14). The share of direct investment by the oil and chemicals sectors in the United Kingdom as well as in Ireland and Denmark increased, which was due in part to the exploration and exploitation of North Sea oil and gas. On the other hand, these sectors' direct investment in major European investment destinations, such as the Federal Republic of Germany, France, and Belgium and Luxembourg, showed a very marked decrease. The combined share of these countries in total outward direct investment declined from over 8 % in 1973 to just under 5 % in 1983.

The decline of direct investment in these European countries must be viewed in the light of the overcapacity confronting the oil and chemical industries. Owing in part to the oil crisis of 1973-1974, the mid-1970s witnessed the emergence of substantial overcapacity in the oil industry, leading to shrivelling profit margins and declining investment activity, especially in Europe. It was notably this factor which accounted for the relative decline in direct investment in the years 1976-1978. Although some subsequent recovery has been apparent, a situation of overcapacity has persisted to date.

Thus, according to data of the European Commission, some 844 million metric tons of oil were processed in the EC as a whole in the peak year 1977. In early 1985 this amount had decreased by nearly 31 % to 583 million metric tons. At the end of 1984 the degree of utilization of total refining capacity in the Communities averaged 72 %.[31] In the Western European countries, the past decade has seen the close-down

[31] A similar development has occurred in the Netherlands; however, the Netherlands has also seen substantial investment to upgrade (conversion) capacity (section 7.2).

of some eighty refineries. Consequently, it is not to be expected that the direct investment flows in this sector in Europe will re-attain the high level of ten years ago. Moreover, as reported in Petroleum Intelligence Weekly, the international oil groups would appear to be increasing their orientation towards the United States for reasons of profitability.

In addition to these factors, other influences of a structural nature are making themselves felt on the destination and volume of direct investment. For instance, oil and gas exploitation used to be concentrated in a limited number of geographical locations. Nowadays, oil and gas exploration is taking place all over the world. In addition to major projects and acquisitions in the United States and the developing countries of Asia, the operations of Netherlands enterprises in such areas as Latin America may be mentioned in this context. The downstream operations, too, are increasingly performed in regional production and refining centres. The last link in the chain, the chemical industry, is also on the eve of greater geographical distribution. Thus, in the future some OPEC countries, too, will certainly enter the market as suppliers of oil derivatives and (bulk) chemicals.[32] For instance, the increase in refining capacity between 1984 and 1990 in Saudi Arabia, Kuwait and Libya alone is estimated at 60 million metric tons.

A much sharper turning-away from Europe on a much broader front was apparent in the metal and food industries. Within the metal industry, the share of the EC in total outward direct investment was more than halved, from 15 % to 6 %, and in the food industry the EC share decreased from 8 % to slightly less than 3 %; this investment even declined in absolute terms (Chart 15). It thus disappeared from the top ten in the list of direct investment by country/sector. Whereas in 1973 direct investment in EC countries by the metal and food industries held four positions in the top ten, in 1983 these positions had been taken over by other investment, including that by the metal and food industries (and services) in the United States (Table 14).

Within the *metal* industry, especially the decrease in the share of direct investment in the Federal Republic of Germany was a striking phenomenon. This decrease was primarily due to the break-up of transnational units owing to unsuccessful Netherlands-German cooperation in iron and steel-making and in aircraft manufacture. Additionally, more generally within Europe, the movements in sales and profitability in this sector have been most disappointing, as was also evident from the calculations of return rates. Furthermore, this sector was hard hit by heavy competition from Japan and other countries from the Far East, ranging from shipbuilding to the photographic industry and consumer electronics. This has already given rise to defensive

---

[32] However, the EC is considering to protect the domestic markets for refined oil products, Het Financieele Dagblad, November 30, 1984.

Table 13
Breakdown of Netherlands direct investment abroad, 1973 and 1983
(% of total)

Country or group of countries/sector	Production industries					
	mining and quarrying, oil and chemicals			metals and electrical engineering		
	1973	1983	Δ	1973	1983	Δ
France	2.27	1.26	-1.00	1.74	0.95	-0.79
Belgium and Luxembourg	1.52	1.16	-0.35	2.35	1.46	-0.88
Federal Republic of Germany	4.41	2.55	-1.86	7.42	1.64	-5.78
Italy	0.44	0.17	-0.27	0.53	0.54	0.01
United Kingdom	10.79	14.34	3.55	2.70	1.25	-1.45
Ireland	0.14	1.21	1.07	0.05	0.05	–
Denmark	0.43	0.90	0.47	0.11	0.06	-0.05
EC	20.01	21.59	1.59	14.90	5.96	-8.94
United States	9.93	15.92	5.99	1.64	3.09	1.45
Switzerland	0.42	0.58	0.17	0.12	0.74	0.63
Other developed countries	8.88	8.08	-0.80	2.78	1.85	-0.93
Developing countries						
Europe	1.23	0.42	-0.81	0.93	0.46	-0.47
Africa	-0.65	0.96	1.61	0.10	0.07	-0.04
Asia	2.34	3.29	0.96	0.92	0.88	-0.04
Latin America	5.19	2.42	-2.78	2.68	1.35	-1.33
(of which: Netherlands Antilles)	(2.34)	(0.90)	(-1.44)	(0.70)	(0.27)	(-0.43)
Total developing countries	8.11	7.09	-1.02	4.64	2.76	-1.88
Grand total	47.35	53.26	5.92	24.07	14.40	-9.67

[1] Including agriculture and fishing, and construction.

acquisitions and forms of cooperation within Europe. Finally, the European multinational enterprises are complaining increasingly about the lack of European unity and cooperation; fears are even being expressed that these European multinationals might disappear in the continued absence of European unity.[33]

The shift in Netherlands investors' preference from the EC towards the United States is also apparent in the *food* industry. In this sector, too, the Western European consumer market is characterized by 'pronounced congestion phenomena'; rewards are meagre and incentives to maintain a presence are diminishing.[34] Moreover, in

[33] Het Financieele Dagblad, April 26, 1985.
[34] FEM-trends, April 13, 1985.

food, drink and tobacco			other [1]			total		
1973	1983	Δ	1973	1983	Δ	1973	1983	Δ
1.19	0.59	-0.60	0.27	0.11	-0.15	5.46	2.91	-2.55
0.80	0.56	-0.24	0.74	0.61	-0.14	5.41	3.79	-1.62
4.95	1.00	-3.95	0.27	0.23	-0.04	17.05	5.41	-11.64
0.54	0.39	-0.15	0.12	0.01	-0.11	1.63	1.11	-0.52
0.26	0.13	-0.13	0.71	0.29	-0.42	14.46	16.01	1.55
0.03	0.06	0.03	0.01	0.01	-0.01	0.24	1.33	1.09
0.16	0.05	-0.11	0.03	-0.01	-0.04	0.73	1.01	0.27
7.93	2.78	-5.15	2.15	1.25	-0.91	44.99	31.58	-13.41
1.78	2.16	0.37	-0.02	0.45	0.47	13.34	21.62	8.28
0.55	0.94	0.39	0.23	0.27	0.03	1.32	2.53	1.21
0.85	0.41	-0.44	0.26	0.18	-0.08	12.77	10.52	-2.25
0.53	0.28	-0.24	0.06	0.02	-0.04	2.74	1.19	-1.55
0.49	0.10	-0.40	0.28	0.16	-0.12	0.23	1.28	1.05
0.45	0.50	0.05	0.01	-0.22	-0.23	3.72	4.45	0.73
0.68	0.57	-0.10	0.25	1.02	0.76	8.80	5.36	-3.45
(0.48)	(0.14)	(-0.34)	(0.20)	(0.89)	(0.69)	(3.72)	(2.21)	(-1.52)
2.15	1.45	-0.70	0.60	0.98	0.38	15.50	12.28	-3.22
13.27	7.74	-5.53	3.23	3.12	-0.11	87.92	78.53	-9.39

recent years the food industry has been endeavouring to strengthen further its position in the United States, seeking notably to complement existing operations without straying too much from its traditional production pattern.

Except for the transport, storage and communication sector, the share of *services* in outward direct investment increased sharply across the board, thus improving the position of services in the list of direct investment. Whereas in the production industries some multinational enterprises shrivelled to become little more than national enterprises, many national enterprises in services evolved into full-fledged multinationals. Notably the United States was a major investment destination, especially in the

Table 13 (continued)
Breakdown of Netherlands direct investment abroad, 1973 and 1983
(% of total)

Country or group of countries/sector	Services					
	trade			transport, storage and communication		
	1973	1983	Δ	1973	1983	Δ
France	0.59	0.64	0.05	0.12	0.07	-0.05
Belgium and Luxembourg	0.77	0.82	0.05	0.25	0.17	-0.08
Federal Republic of Germany	1.20	0.52	-0.68	0.17	0.10	-0.07
Italy	0.13	0.12	-0.01	0.01	–	-0.01
United Kingdom	0.35	0.40	0.05	0.16	0.06	-0.10
Ireland	–	0.01	0.01	–	–	–
Denmark	0.04	0.04	-0.01	–	–	–
EC	3.09	2.55	-0.54	0.71	0.40	-0.31
United States	0.55	1.25	0.70	-0.01	0.25	0.25
Switzerland	0.57	0.83	0.26	0.09	0.09	–
Other developed countries	0.17	0.37	0.20	0.26	–	-0.26
Developing countries						
Europe	0.02	0.04	0.01	0.01	–	-0.01
Africa	0.15	0.08	-0.08	0.06	0.01	-0.05
Asia	0.10	0.15	0.05	0.06	0.15	0.09
Latin America	0.69	2.30	1.62	1.79	0.32	-1.47
(of which: Netherlands Antilles)	(0.38)	(1.89)	(1.51)	(1.15)	(0.29)	(-0.87)
Total developing countries	0.97	2.57	1.60	1.91	0.48	-1.43
Grand total	5.35	7.57	2.22	2.97	1.22	-1.75

second half of the period. Additionally, Switzerland and the developing countries of Asia were favourite destinations. For the EC the pattern was not clear-cut: in the 'older' trade sector, the share of the EC declined, whereas the much more recent multinationalization of the Netherlands banking and insurance sector and of the other services sector (mainly investment and real estate companies) prompted relatively higher direct investment in Europe. These developments are aptly illustrated by the shifts in the list of outward direct investment by country/sector. Whereas in 1973 the list did not include any of the services sectors, in 1983 services accounted for three positions in the top ten: other services and banking and insurance in the United States and trade in the Netherlands Antilles. In the 'growth list' – showing the positions exhibiting the highest growth rates – services also accounted for three positions.

anking and insurance			other			total			Grand total		
973	1983	Δ	1973	1983	Δ	1973	1983	Δ	1973	1983	Δ
.06	0.06	–	0.15	0.30	0.15	0.91	1.07	0.15	6.37	3.98	-2.39
.46	0.79	0.33	0.19	0.65	0.45	1.68	2.43	0.75	7.09	6.22	-0.87
.14	0.44	0.30	0.28	0.50	0.22	1.79	1.56	-0.23	18.84	6.98	-11.87
–	0.03	0.03	0.05	0.11	0.06	0.18	0.25	0.07	1.82	1.36	-0.45
.21	0.45	0.24	0.20	0.65	0.46	0.92	1.56	0.64	15.38	17.57	2.19
.02	0.01	–	–	0.02	0.02	0.03	0.05	0.02	0.27	1.38	1.11
–	0.04	0.04	–	–	–	0.05	0.08	0.03	0.78	1.09	0.31
.89	1.82	0.93	0.88	2.24	1.36	5.57	7.01	1.44	50.56	38.59	-11.97
.08	2.50	2.41	0.07	2.25	2.18	0.69	6.24	5.55	14.04	27.86	13.82
.16	0.42	0.26	0.18	0.66	0.48	1.00	2.00	1.01	2.32	4.54	2.22
.72	0.58	-0.14	0.01	0.11	0.09	1.18	1.07	-0.11	13.94	11.58	-2.36
–	0.03	0.03	0.02	0.10	0.08	0.06	0.17	0.11	2.80	1.36	-1.44
.01	0.01	-0.01	–	0.03	0.03	0.22	0.12	-0.11	0.46	1.40	0.95
.05	0.34	0.29	0.01	0.03	0.03	0.21	0.67	0.46	3.93	5.12	1.19
.21	0.46	0.25	0.46	1.12	0.66	3.14	4.19	1.05	11.95	9.55	-2.40
.19)	(0.40)	(0.20)	(0.38)	(1.06)	(0.68)	(2.11)	(3.63)	(1.52)	(5.83)	(5.84)	(0.01)
.27	0.83	0.56	0.48	1.27	0.79	3.64	5.15	1.51	19.14	17.43	-1.70
2.13	6.14	4.01	1.63	6.53	4.91	12.08	21.47	9.39	100.00	100.00	–

The cross-border development of Netherlands services is to be regarded as a logical element in the upgrading process which is leading the Netherlands economy towards a high degree of specialization and service-intensity. An important motive force underlying the multinationalization is the urge to increase the scale of operation. With regard to both (retail) trade and banking and insurance, enterprises conclude that the Netherlands market is limited in terms of volume and is becoming increasingly saturated. It is, for instance, reported that ongoing large-scale investment in retail trade in the Netherlands would have a destructive rather than constructive effect. Moreover, some retailing enterprises have outgrown the size of the Netherlands market, so that the expansionary urge has had to be deflected in part towards other countries. A case in point is the United States, which offers foreign investors

Table 14
Netherlands direct investment abroad, ranked by country and sector

Rank	By country			By sector			By country and sector		
	1973	1983	Δ	1973	1983	Δ	1973	1983	Δ
1	D	US	US	OC	OC	OC	UK/OC	US/OC	US/OC
2	UK	UK	UK	ME	ME	OS	US/OC	UK/OC	UK/OC
3	US	OD	OD	FO	FO	TR	OD/OC	OD/OC	OD/OC
4	OD	D	AN	TR	TR	ME	D/ME	AS/OC	US/ME
5	BL	BL	CH	TC	OS	BI	D/FO	US/ME	US/BI
6	F	AN	AS	BI	BI	FO	D/OC	D/OC	AS/OC
7	LA	AS	BL	OI	OI	CI	LA/OC	US/BI	US/OS
8	AN	CH	F	OS	TC	OI	OD/ME	US/OS	AN/TR
9	AS	F	LA	CI	CI	AG	UK/ME	US/FO	US/FO
10	EU	LA	IR	AG	AG	TC	BL/ME	AN/TR	AF/OC

Legend:
US = United States
UK = United Kingdom
D = Federal Republic of Germany
BL = Belgium and Luxembourg
F = France
IR = Ireland
CH = Switzerland
OD = Other developed countries
EU = Developing countries in Europe
LA = Developing countries in Latin America (excluding Netherlands Antilles)
AS = Developing countries in Asia
AF = Developing countries in Africa
AN = Netherlands Antilles

Legend:
OC = Mining and quarrying, oil and chemicals
ME = Metals and electrical engineering
FO = Food, drink and tobacco
OI = Other production industries
TR = Trade
TC = Transport, storage and communication
BI = Banking and insurance
OS = Other services
CI = Construction
AG = Agriculture and fishing

easy access and a good business climate (cf. section 6.1.2). Additionally, an important strategic variable is the drive to expand the existing national range of services so as to be able to offer a mix of cross-border services of international sophistication.[35]

For the insurance sector, too, it is reported that the Netherlands does not offer any further significant growth opportunities. Netherlands consumers are rated as 'highly' insured compared with consumers in other countries, so that the market is saturated and characterized by keen competition. The second reason listed for the internationalization drive is the wish to achieve a better spread of political and insurance risks: 'it doesn't rain everywhere at the same time'. Again, the United States is a favourite

[35] Cf. Radio news commentary 'Hier en Nu', February 18, 1981.

investment destination, which is easily accessible to foreign investors. Apart from the general pulling forces referred to earlier, a role is played here by the fact that the United States accounts for 50 % of the world insurance market (against a mere 2 % for the Netherlands). Moreover, market growth is expected to centre on the United States, considering the low average age of the population, its insurance tradition and its increasing insurance-mindedness. The pace of the multinationalization in the past ten years may be illustrated by the fact that several Netherlands enterprises already derive more than half their premium income from foreign countries, notably North America, which is thus rapidly becoming their second home market.[36] More recently attention was also directed towards Japan, where the Netherlands was the first European country to gain a foothold. A unique feature of the insurance sector's penetration into Japan is the cooperation with the oil sector, with petrol stations being used as sales offices for insurance. Such investment is, incidentally, reckoned to need seven or eight years before break-even point is reached and to involve pay-back periods of some twelve years.[37]

In other services – mainly investment and real estate companies – similar acquisitions and tendencies are discernible. Information services also deserve to be mentioned in this context.

The internationalization of the banking system dates from a much more distant past; the banks followed in the wake of Netherlands traders and responded to the needs of the internationally operating enterprises. However, in the late 1970s and the early 1980s in particular this internationalization was given a broader base. Furthermore, like other markets, the financial markets are progressively evolving into a single financial world market, and banks aim at establishing a full presence in the major financial centres.[38]

It might be noted, though, that the balance-of-payments figures for recent years would suggest that the enormous expansion of direct investment by the services sector has levelled off somewhat in favour of the production industries (Table 15). As this expansion notably concerned direct investment by banking and insurance in the United States, it might be possible that the sharp increase in the dollar's exchange rate has had the effect of slowing down such investment, after the dollar's relatively very low value had been a major investment incentive until the early 1980s. Presumably, the services sector is still more 'guilder-based' and hence more sensitive to changes in the dollar/guilder rate than the production industries, which succeeded in 1983 in recovering part of the ground lost in the United States. Furthermore, it is probable that, after its strong expansion in the United States, the services sector is 'taking a breather' and will increasingly concentrate on stimulating the autonomous growth of their newly acquired interests.

---

36 Cf. 'Overzeese ambities', NRC Supplement, June 5, 1985.

37 De Volkskrant, October 1, 1985.

38 Het Financieele Dagblad, September 18, 1985.

Table 15
Outward direct investment, broken down by sector
(balance-of-payments flows; billions of guilders)

Sector	1982	1983	1984
Agriculture and fishing	–	–	–
Production industries			
– mining and quarrying, oil and chemicals	2.8	2.1	5.5
– metals and electrical engineering	–0.8	0.5	0.3
– food, drink and tobacco	0.2	0.2	0.6
– other	0.1	–	0.2
Total production industries	2.3	2.8	6.6
Construction	0.1	–0.1	0.2
Services			
– trade	0.8	0.7	0.2
– transport, storage and communication	0.1	–	0.1
– banking and insurance	1.5	0.9	0.8
– other	0.6	0.5	0.5
Total services	3.0	2.1	1.6
Grand total	5.4	4.8	8.4
(as % of national income)	(1.6)	(1.4)	(2.4)

In summary, it may be noted that the future may be expected to see a wide-ranging continuation of the expansion of Netherlands outward direct investment. On the one hand, the domestic 'propelling forces' – in the form of healthy large enterprises having ownership advantages capable of being internalized – are strong and now also extend to the services sector. On the other hand, the 'pulling forces' have increased materially; cases in point are location advantages elsewhere as reflected in market size and uniformity, relative profitability and costs and possibly, to an increasing extent, tariff differentials ensuing from protectionist measures. Considering this, prospects would appear to be for increasing specialization along the lines of the comparative advantages of the various countries (see also section 7.2).

7.1.2 Foreign direct investment in the Netherlands

Apart from some differences in emphasis, the composition and structural development of inward direct investment were marked by the same trends as those of outward direct investment:

- Here, too, the share of the production industries showed a decline, in this case from nearly 75 % to nearly 60 %. The decline was thus even sharper than for outward direct investment, albeit that in 1983 some redress was apparent (Chart 16).
- The decrease in the share of the production industries was likewise wholly offset by the services sectors, which accounted for as much as 42 % of total inward direct investment in 1983.
- The share of the EC in inward direct investment also fell sharply (from 43 % to 31 %), but in this case the decrease was notably in favour of the share of the group of other countries and not of the United States. However, this development caused the shares of the various countries in inward direct investment to tend towards the same ratio as for outward direct investment: one-third for the EC, one-third for the United States and one-third for the other countries (Table 16).

Inspection of the invested amounts given in Table 16 and Chart 17 shows that for inward direct investment, too, the largest invested amount per country/sector was accounted for by the combination the United States/*oil and chemicals.* Both in 1973 and in 1983, this combination held pride of place within inward direct investment. Moreover, it also showed the largest increase in absolute terms; see Table 17. Nevertheless, US direct investment in oil and chemicals declined relative to that in other sectors. The same was true of the EC and the other developed countries. It was only direct investment from the developing countries of Asia and Latin America in Netherlands oil and chemicals which recorded a slight relative increase. The overall share of oil and chemicals decreased by nearly 10 percentage points to 32 % of total inward direct investment. It may be expected that, for as long as the overcapacity in the oil and chemical industries in the Netherlands (and in the other European countries) persists, this relative decrease will continue, despite substantial capital-deepening investment in these industries for the upgrading of production processes; it might be noted that its comparative advantages in this area give the Netherlands a relatively favourable position compared with most of the other EC countries (section 7.2).

The share of *metals and electrical engineering* in total inward direct investment also showed a drastic decrease. However, this decrease was less widely distributed among the various countries than in the case of oil and chemicals. It was almost wholly accounted for by direct investment from the Federal Republic of Germany and thus formed the mirror image of developments (break-ups of transnational units, etc.) with

Table 16
Breakdown of foreign direct investment in the Netherlands, 1973 and 1983
(% of total)

Country or group of countries/sector	Production industries					
	mining and quarrying, oil and chemicals			metals and electrical engineering		
	1973	1983	Δ	1973	1983	Δ
France	2.12	0.68	-1.44	0.37	0.72	0.35
Belgium and Luxembourg	1.42	0.52	-0.90	1.60	2.05	0.45
Federal Republic of Germany	1.40	1.40	–	8.62	0.74	-7.88
Italy	0.16	0.15	-0.01	-0.02	–	0.02
United Kingdom	6.55	4.27	-2.28	0.78	0.39	-0.39
Ireland	–	–	–	–	–	–
Denmark	0.01	0.01	–	–	0.02	0.02
EC	11.66	7.03	-4.63	11.36	3.93	-7.43
United States	22.31	20.04	-2.27	4.62	4.70	0.08
Switzerland	3.20	2.80	-0.40	1.63	1.51	-0.11
Japan	–	0.03	0.03	0.06	0.06	–
Other developed countries	0.43	0.29	-0.14	0.79	1.31	0.52
Developing countries						
Europe	–	–	–	–	–	–
Africa	1.90	0.17	-1.73	–	0.01	0.01
Asia	–	0.51	0.51	0.02	0.29	0.27
Latin America	0.76	0.91	0.15	0.61	0.68	0.07
(of which: Netherlands Antilles)	(0.74)	(0.39)	(-0.35)	(0.49)	(0.50)	(0.01)
Total developing countries	2.65	1.59	-1.06	0.63	0.98	0.35
Grand total	40.25	31.78	-8.47	19.08	12.48	-6.59

[1] Including agriculture and fishing, and construction.

regard to outward direct investment. The investment position of the Federal Republic of Germany in these sectors even dropped from a respectable second place in the list of inward direct investment (8.5 % of the total) into relative insignificance (cf. Table 17). However, the share of Belgium and Luxembourg and that of France in inward direct investment in these sectors increased slightly, as did the shares of the group of other developed countries and (again) the developing countries in Asia. These developments would suggest that the Netherlands metals and electrical engineering sectors have succeeded in retaining a measure of relative attractiveness, presumably in the highly developed segments in particular.

food, drink and tobacco			other [1]			total		
1973	1983	Δ	1973	1983	Δ	1973	1983	Δ
0.04	0.01	-0.03	0.68	0.23	-0.45	3.20	1.64	-1.57
0.59	0.18	-0.40	1.43	0.55	-0.88	5.03	3.30	-1.72
0.03	0.08	0.05	0.31	0.30	-0.02	10.36	2.51	-7.85
-	-	-	-	-	-	0.14	0.15	0.01
1.25	1.41	0.16	2.13	1.20	-0.93	10.73	7.28	-3.45
-	-	-	0.01	0.01	-0.01	0.02	0.01	-0.01
-	-	-	0.04	0.08	0.04	0.05	0.11	0.06
1.91	1.68	-0.23	4.61	2.37	-2.24	29.53	15.00	-14.53
1.43	2.41	0.98	1.67	1.01	-0.66	30.03	28.17	-1.87
1.37	1.93	0.55	1.31	1.01	-0.30	7.51	7.25	-0.26
-	-	-	0.02	0.28	0.26	0.08	0.37	0.29
0.17	0.09	-0.07	0.69	0.41	-0.28	2.08	2.10	0.02
-	-	-	-	-	-	-	0.01	0.01
-	-	-	-	-	-	1.90	0.18	-1.72
-	0.04	0.04	-	0.12	0.12	0.02	0.97	0.94
0.64	0.84	0.19	0.34	1.55	1.21	2.35	3.98	1.63
(0.54)	(0.47)	(-0.07)	(0.22)	(1.37)	(1.16)	(1.99)	(2.74)	(0.74)
0.65	0.88	0.23	0.34	1.68	1.34	4.27	5.13	0.86
5.53	6.99	1.46	8.65	6.76	-1.89	73.50	58.01	-15.49

Inward direct investment in the *food* industry developed relatively favourably. Whereas in 1973 the share in total inward direct investment had still been 5.5 %, in 1983 it had increased to 7 %. The increase was notably accounted for by direct investment from the United Kingdom, the United States and Switzerland. Apparently, the investors concerned sought to maintain or establish a presence in the Netherlands food sector. Apart from the wish to gain a foothold within the 'high' EC tariff walls in this area, a role may have been played in this respect by the relatively attractive position which the Netherlands has traditionally held in the agricultural and the food, drink and tobacco sectors. A study made by the German Ministry of Agriculture has,

Table 16 (continued)
Breakdown of foreign direct investment in the Netherlands, 1973 and 1983 (% of total)

Country or group of countries/sector	Services: trade 1973	Services: trade 1983	Services: trade Δ	Services: transport, storage and communication 1973	Services: transport, storage and communication 1983	Services: transport, storage and communication Δ
France	0.47	0.55	0.08	0.04	0.04	–
Belgium and Luxembourg	1.70	0.96	–0.74	0.28	0.07	–0.21
Federal Republic of Germany	1.37	1.37	–0.01	0.51	0.12	–0.38
Italy	0.14	–	–0.14	–	0.02	0.02
United Kingdom	2.34	2.51	0.17	0.43	0.19	–0.23
Ireland	–	–	–	–	–	–
Denmark	–	0.19	0.18	–	–	–
EC	6.04	5.58	–0.46	1.25	0.45	–0.81
United States	3.56	3.43	–0.13	0.03	0.13	0.11
Switzerland	1.49	2.42	0.94	0.19	0.14	–0.05
Japan	0.10	0.73	0.64	0.01	0.01	–
Other developed countries	1.34	0.97	–0.37	0.06	–0.01	–0.08
Developing countries						
Europe	0.03	0.02	–0.01	–	–	–
Africa	0.01	0.08	0.07	0.01	–	–0.01
Asia	0.01	0.08	0.07	–	–	–
Latin America	0.86	5.59	4.73	0.15	0.35	0.19
(of which: Netherlands Antilles)	(0.81)	(4.86)	(4.05)	(–0.08)	(0.33)	(0.41)
Total developing countries	0.91	5.77	4.86	0.17	0.35	0.18
Grand total	13.44	18.91	5.48	1.72	1.07	–0.65

for instance, shown that labour productivity in Netherlands agriculture is the highest in the world. 'The average farmer in the Netherlands produces food for 112 persons'. For the United States this figure is 79 and for the Federal Republic of Germany 62.[39] In this connection, it is significant to note the reasons advanced by a US food producer for establishing an operation in the Netherlands after having made a study of possible locations in eleven countries: 'An important argument was the fact that the Netherlands is an excellent source of the required raw materials, especially dairy products, and that technology here is at a high level. Additionally, Rotterdam is one of the world's most efficient container ports'.[40]

[39] NRC, August 27, 1985.
[40] De Volkskrant, May 19, 1982.

banking and insurance			other			total			Grand total		
973	1983	Δ	1973	1983	Δ	1973	1983	Δ	1973	1983	Δ
).68	1.78	1.10	0.12	0.60	0.48	1.32	2.97	1.65	4.52	4.60	0.08
).22	0.02	-0.20	0.11	0.66	0.55	2.30	1.71	-0.59	7.33	5.01	-2.32
).26	0.28	0.02	0.15	1.26	1.11	2.29	3.03	0.74	12.65	5.54	-7.11
).06	0.07	0.01	0.01	0.07	0.06	0.21	0.16	-0.05	0.35	0.31	-0.04
.43	3.41	0.98	1.85	1.88	0.03	7.05	7.99	0.94	17.77	15.27	-2.50
-	0.03	0.03	0.09	0.38	0.29	0.09	0.41	0.33	0.11	0.42	0.32
-	-	-	-	-	-	-	0.19	0.19	0.05	0.30	0.25
3.64	5.58	1.94	2.32	4.86	2.53	13.26	16.46	3.20	42.79	31.46	-11.33
.11	1.57	0.46	2.48	1.44	-1.04	7.19	6.58	-0.61	37.22	34.74	-2.47
).12	0.05	-0.07	0.56	1.07	0.51	2.36	3.68	1.33	9.87	10.93	1.06
).58	1.35	0.77	-	0.03	0.03	0.69	2.12	1.43	0.77	2.49	1.72
-	0.04	0.05	0.06	0.85	0.79	1.46	1.85	0.39	3.54	3.95	0.42
).01	0.06	0.05	-	0.02	0.02	0.05	0.10	0.05	0.05	0.11	0.06
-	-	-	-	-	-	0.02	0.08	0.06	1.92	0.26	-1.66
).18	0.49	0.30	0.02	0.02	-	0.22	0.60	0.37	0.25	1.56	1.31
).01	0.12	0.11	0.23	4.46	4.22	1.25	10.51	9.25	3.60	14.49	10.88
(-)	(0.07)	(0.07)	(0.20)	(4.12)	(3.92)	(0.93)	(9.38)	(8.45)	(2.92)	(12.12)	(9.20)
).20	0.67	0.47	0.26	4.49	4.24	1.54	11.29	9.74	5.81	16.42	10.60
5.65	9.26	3.61	5.69	12.74	7.05	26.50	41.99	15.49	100.00	100.00	-

The share of the *other* production industries (paper, textiles, etc., including construction and agriculture) in inward direct investment from the developed countries in particular, except Japan, showed a decline. Only in inward direct investment from the developing countries of Asia did the share of these sector exhibit a slight increase; with regard to direct investment from Latin America, the picture was heavily dominated by the Netherlands Antilles.

On the whole, the development of foreign direct investment in the Netherlands *services* sectors was fairly auspicious. This is also reflected in the list of inward direct investment by country/sector: whereas in 1973 the top ten had included four positions held by services, in 1983 this had increased to six, against only four for the pro-

Table 17
Foreign direct investment in the Netherlands, ranked by country and sector

Rank	By country			By sector			By country and sector		
	1973	1983	Δ	1973	1983	Δ	1973	1983	Δ
1	US	US	US	OC	OC	OC	US/OC	US/OC	US/OC
2	UK	UK	AN	ME	TR	TR	D/ME	AN/TR	AN/TR
3	D	AN	UK	TR	OS	OS	UK/OC	US/ME	AN/OS
4	CH	CH	CH	OI	ME	BI	US/ME	UK/OC	US/ME
5	BL	D	F	OS	BI	ME	US/TR	AN/OS	UK/BI
6	F	BL	OD	BI	FO	FO	CH/OC	US/TR	US/TR
7	OD	F	JA	FO	OI	AG	US/OS	UK/BI	US/FO
8	AN	OB	BL	TC	TC	OI	UK/BI	CH/OC	CH/TR
9	AF	JA	LA	CI	AG	CI	UK/TR	UK/TR	UK/OC
10	JA	LA	AS	AG	CI	TC	F/OC	CH/TR	UK/TR

Legend:
US = United States
UK = United Kingdom
D = Federal Republic of Germany
BL = Belgium and Luxembourg
F = France
CH = Switzerland
JA = Japan
OD = Other developed countries
LA = Developing countries in Latin America (excluding Netherlands Antilles)
AS = Developing countries in Asia
AF = Developing countries in Africa
AN = Netherlands Antilles

Legend:
OC = Mining and quarrying, oil and chemicals
ME = Metals and electrical engineering
FO = Food, drink and tobacco
OI = Other production industries
TR = Trade
TC = Transport, storage and communication
BI = Banking and insurance
OS = Other services
CI = Construction
AG = Agriculture and fishing

duction industries (Table 17). Of the six positions held by services, four related to *trade.* Notably trade investment from the United Kingdom, the United States, Switzerland and the Netherlands Antilles was substantial, leading to improvements in the relative positions of most of these countries. Trade investment from Japan and the developing countries of Asia and Latin America (excluding the Netherlands Antilles) also developed favourably, while that from France and Denmark showed a slight improvement in relative terms. Presumably, this attractiveness of the Netherlands for foreign trade investment has been underlain by a number of specific 'pulling forces':

- Considering its geographical location and excellent infrastructure and communication facilities, many foreign enterprises regard the Netherlands as the 'gateway to Europe'.
- The working population is highly skilled, traditionally stable and internationally oriented.

- The Netherlands has a strong tradition of free trade, as regards both visible trade and capital movements.
- Over the past five years, the increase in wage costs has been about 20 % less than in the principal other industrialized countries, a factor of major importance for the labour-intensive sectors in particular.
- Generally, foreign enterprises operating in the Netherlands market achieve high rates of return.
- In a number of respects, Netherlands tax legislation favours the establishment of international enterprises.[41]

In the past few years these factors have contributed to the establishment of some twenty distribution companies and reinvoicing companies, of which about half are of US and a quarter of Japanese origin.

The depressed situation with regard to inward direct investment in the *transport and storage* sector proves to extend to almost all investing countries. This illustrates the structural aspect of developments in this sector (compare also the depressed situation regarding outward direct investment). However, the share of *banking and insurance* increased substantially, to nearly 10 % of total inward direct investment. Higher shares were notably recorded for France, the United Kingdom, Japan, the United States and (again) the developing countries of Asia. The liberal admission policy pursued by the Netherlands and the fact that this sector tends to follow the trade flows and trading companies have played a major role in this respect. Inward direct investment in other services also developed favourably on a fairly wide front, though distributed somewhat differently among the various investing countries.

In summary, it may be concluded that the total change in inward direct investment, too, was to a major extent due to investment in *oil and chemicals.* However, the relative importance of these sectors declined; in view of the vast amounts traditionally involved in investment in these sectors, this caused overall inward direct investment to be somewhat depressed. More recent figures for the inward *flows* also indicate that in these sectors funds are being repatriated rather than invested. This is notably due to specific developments within US oil companies (tight cash position), while, moreover, the wide interest rate differentials have siphoned off funds through intra-group current accounts (Table 18). Yet, considering its specific comparative advantages in these sectors, the Netherlands definitely has no structurally weak position in this respect (section 7.2).

Regarding inward direct investment in the metal industry, this sector probably offers fairly favourable prospects after the large-scale restructuring in the 1970s. The same is true, to a much greater extent, of the Netherlands food industry, which has acquired an indisputably strong position in the world and offers foreign enterprises

[41] Cf. Andriessen, *op. cit.*

Table 18
Inward direct investment, broken down by sector
(balance-of-payments flows; billions of guilders)

Sector	1982	1983	1984
Agriculture and fishing	–	–	–
Production industries			
– mining and quarrying, oil and chemicals	–0.3	–0.4	–0.4
– metals and electrical engineering	0.3	0.3	0.8
– food, drink and tobacco	0.2	0.4	0.5
– other	0.1	0.2	0.1
Total production industries	0.3	0.5	1.0
Construction	–	–	0.1
Services			
– trade	1.1	0.7	–0.2
– transport, storage and communication	0.1	–	0.1
– banking and insurance	0.1	0.3	0.2
– other	0.3	0.5	0.4
Total services	1.6	1.5	0.5
Grand total	1.9	2.0	1.6
(as % of national income)	(0.6)	(0.6)	(0.4)

major incentives for setting up operations in this country. With regard to the trade sector and, more generally, the financial sectors, a number of favourable factors place the Netherlands in a promising position. (Note: the 1984 flow figure in the trade sector was negative owing to non-recurrent large repayments of intra-group loans.) In geographical terms, emphasis in inward direct investment will presumably undergo some shift from the 'traditional' investors such as the EC countries and the United States to such countries as Japan and the developing countries of Southeast Asia.[42]

7.2 Specialization

The percentage shares given in Table 13 and Chart 15 show that in 1983 more than one-half of Netherlands outward direct investment was accounted for by oil and chemicals (nearly 53.5 %). The comparable shares for the United States and the

[42] FEM, Gevecht om de wereldmarkt, September 7, 1985.

Federal Republic of Germany were 38.4 % and 23.8 %, respectively. As the relevant share is much higher for Netherlands outward direct investment, our country may be termed relatively 'specialized' in these sectors compared to the United States and the Federal Republic of Germany. An interesting question is to what extent the Netherlands also has a relative 'investment specialization' in other sectors.

To afford an insight into this subject, so-called specialization coefficients have been calculated for direct investment.[43] In the example given above, this coefficient would be $\frac{53.5}{38.4} = 1.39$ relative to the United States and $\frac{53.5}{23.8} = 2.25$ relative to the Federal Republic of Germany.

As in both cases the coefficient exceeds one, Netherlands outward direct investment may be called relatively specialized in oil and chemicals compared to the United States and the Federal Republic of Germany.

Such calculations are to some extent hampered by the fact that the underlying figures are either by necessity fairly aggregated or are not based on uniform definitions in the various countries. Table 19 shows qualitative indications of the specialization coefficients for direct investment relative to the United States and the Federal Republic of Germany, two countries for which the relevant data are fully available.

It is evident from Table 19 that Netherlands *outward* direct investment relative to *both* countries is specialized in oil and chemicals and in food. The metal industry is relatively strongly represented in outward direct investment compared to the United States; however, this is not so compared to the Federal Republic of Germany, where the metal industry traditionally holds a strong position. On the other hand, the fact that the Netherlands is more of a trading nation than the Federal Republic of Germany is evident from its relatively larger share of trade in total outward direct investment. Finally, outward direct investment by the Netherlands insurance sector has expanded so rapidly that in 1983 the share of this investment exceeded the comparable share in US outward direct investment. The share of the insurance sector approached the comparable share in the Federal Republic of Germany, though not sufficiently to merit the label 'specialized'.

[43] The coefficient is defined as follows:

$$S_{jk} = \frac{I_{jk}}{I_j} : \frac{I_{nk}}{I_n}$$

where:

I_{jk} = direct investment position of country j in sector k;
I_j = direct investment position of country j in all sectors;
I_{nk} = direct investment position of reference country n in sector k;
I_n = direct investment position of reference country n in all sectors.

If the coefficient exceeds one, the country is relatively 'specialized'.

Table 19
Direct investment specialization of the Netherlands compared with the United States and the Federal Republic of Germany

Sector	Outward				Inward			
	USA		FRG		USA		FRG	
	1981	1983	1981	1983	1981	1983	1981	1983
Production industries	x	x	x	x	x	x	x	x
of which: oil and chemicals	x	x	x	x	x	x	x	x
metals	x	x	o	o	x	x	o	o
food	x	x	x	x	x	x	x	x
other	o	o	o	o	o	o	o	o
Services	o	o	o	o	o	o	o	o
of which: trade	o	o	x	x	x	x	x	x
transport, storage, etc.	o	o	o	o	o	o	o	o
insurance	o	x	o	o	o	o	o	o
banking	o	o	o	o	o	o	o	o

Explanatory note:
x means specialized and o non-specialized compared with the United States or the Federal Republic of Germany.

Regarding the specialization of *inward* direct investment – the 'direct investment dependence' – the close resemblance with outward direct investment is conspicuous in the case of the production industries. This pattern is the more striking if it is realized that goods trade shows comparable similarities in the composition of exports and imports.[44] In this connection, attention may be drawn to the figures from the empirical literature about *intra*-industry trade, which show that the Netherlands ranks high in this respect.[45]

With regard to this complementarity of the Netherlands international goods specialization and the Netherlands international direct investment specialization, it might be noted that in the Netherlands the industrial sectors mentioned include strong multinational enterprises. These enterprises have apparently benefitted from the comparative advantages which the Netherlands had and still has in this respect, advantages which have, in turn, attracted foreign direct investors. The fact that Netherlands goods trade is concentrated on these very sectors would appear to be a

[44] M. van Nieuwkerk, N.P. Driesprong and A.C.J. Stokman, *Aspecten van de Nederlandse betalingsbalans*, Economisch Statistische Berichten 67, nr. 3381, November 17, 1982.

[45] See, for instance, H.B. Grubel and P.J. Lloyd, *Intra-industry trade: The theory and measurement of international trade in differentiated products*, Wiley, New York, 1975.
See also A. Acquino, *Intra-industry trade and inter-industry specialization as concurrent sources of international trade in manufactures*, Weltwirtschaftliches Archiv, 1978, pp. 275-296.

logical consequence. These considerations give rise to the question whether Netherlands international goods trade and Netherlands international direct investment show a complementary relationship, a substitutional relationship or no relationship at all. A precise answer is not possible, because generally the required statistics originate from too many different sources, giving rise to statistical distortions. Hence, it is not possible to draw any firm conclusions about the relationship between production, exports and direct investment. Consequently, only a few aspects of this relationship will be dealt with very briefly.

First, it may be noted that, if an enterprise decides to undertake production in another country (instead of exporting to it), such a decision will frequently concern only part of its exports. It will, for instance, continue to serve nearby markets from its principal establishment, while the more distant markets can be covered (more efficiently and perhaps on a larger scale) by the new production location.

Additionally, it is logical to assume that enterprises producing in various countries will suit the pattern of production to the comparative advantages and disadvantages of the countries concerned. Research into the operations of US parent companies and those of their subsidiaries abroad has shown that these operations are complementary rather than duplicative.[46] Furthermore, studies have shown that notably multinational enterprises from highly developed countries exhibit a tendency towards process and/or product specialization so as to be able to profit from economies of scale and to suit production optimally to widely fluctuating consumer requirements.[47]

Marina v. N. Whitman gives a clear example with regard to the car industry.[48] She points to the development of the 'world car' concept, where cars vary slightly in size and design from one geographical area to the other, but whose parts are highly standardized and interchangeable. She also points out that, in the future, trade in (car) parts might show a higher growth rate than that in finished products. Firstly, the pressure of competition calls for optimum distribution of production. Secondly, there is growing opposition to imports of the car industry's finished products, which are of essential importance for many countries. Thirdly, the post-war trade liberalization has encouraged intra-industry trade. In this context, it is interesting to note that intra-group deliveries of multinational enterprises are estimated to make up between 20 % and 30 % of world trade – a share which is still increasing.[49] Furthermore, out of

---

[46] Cf. I.B. Kravis and R.E. Lipsey, *The location of overseas production and production for export by US multinational firms,* Journal of International Economics, no. 12, 1982.

[47] Cf. J.H. Dunning, *A note on intra-industry foreign direct investment,* Quarterly Review, Banco Nazionale Del Lavoro, December 1982.

[48] Marina v. N. Whitman, *International trade and investment: two perspectives,* Essays in International Finance, no. 143, Princeton, New Jersey, July 1981.

[49] Cf. D.J. Goldsbrough, *International trade of multinational corporations and its responsiveness to changes in aggregate demand and relative prices,* IMF Staff Papers, no. 3, 1981, pp. 573-599.

total US imports from the OECD countries, 54 % originates from enterprises which are affiliated with US multinationals.[50]

The pronounced Netherlands tendency towards intra-industry trade, as shown by Acquino, could also be related to such process and/or product specialization, emphasis here being traditionally less on the car industry (although the parts industry is expanding strongly [51]) and more on the oil and chemical industries, the food industry and the electrical engineering industry.

With regard to the specialization in *oil and chemicals,* it may be noted that for these industries the Netherlands offers distinct comparative advantages. The favourable location and the sound infrastructure of the Netherlands (including large and well-equipped ports) are factors which have favoured the establishment of large petrochemical complexes in this country. An added factor is the availability of oil and gas resources. Apart from the close-down of obsolete refineries, our country is also witnessing a switch towards modern flexible cracking processes; thus production is shifting from bulk products towards oil and chemical specialties (upgrading). This has already given rise to a number of major investment projects, all of which have led to diversification of the product range. The oil crises of 1973 and 1979-1980 have led to an important shift in demand from fuel oil towards lighter products. Total refining capacity in the Netherlands, too, was admittedly too large, but on the other hand very major investments have been made, and are still being made, in upgrading and expanding conversion capacity. This development not only leads to more flexible and more varied production processes, it also enables producers to seek better complementarity to other refineries at home and abroad. Another, related choice is that between in-house production and the cheaper procurement of products from the ever larger and more specialized spot markets. This may result in imports of such specialties, followed by exports as part of a complete product range.

Other examples are provided by the *metal* industry, notably the electrical engineering industry. This industry numbers several so-called centres of competence, which are distributed world-wide and where an enterprise – if it wishes to remain in the forefront of developments – must have a presence. The location policy is reportedly underlain by the principle that the geographical distribution of investment must be such as to give access to the world's foremost markets and technological centres. In this connection, the Far East is seen as the centre for consumer electronics, the United States as the centre for professional products and systems and the Netherlands as the centre for all electric-light operations.[52] It is self-evident that, in the wake of this

[50] Cf. D. van den Bulcke, *Intragroepshandel van multinationale ondernemingen: empirische gegevens en handelspolitieke gevolgen,* Maandschrift Economie, Jaargang 49, 1985, pp. 113-131.

[51] Cf. *Nederland in onderdelen,* Intermediair 43, October 25, 1985.

[52] Het Financieele Dagblad, April 26, 1985.

functional world-wide specialization of production, product trade is concentrated among these centres. Furthermore, on account of certain centres of competence, the Netherlands is an attractive location for foreign enterprises. Another example from this industry is provided by the reciprocal investments of US and European enterprises in the area of electronics. In recent years, the development of digital techniques in electronics has centred on the United States, while the most recent advances in the area of analog techniques have been made in Europe. The reciprocal investments have narrowed the gap between analog and digital techniques, leading to further innovations.[53]

An example of the specialization of the *food* industry is provided by the recent take-over of a UK enterprise by a Netherlands food multinational. Increasing the scale of operations – formerly an important argument for mergers – was reportedly not a major motive for this acquisition. The fact is that technological advances have permitted the manufacture of more flexible machinery suitable for a variety of products. A more important argument was the expected synergistic effect, in terms of both geographical complementarity and know-how.[54] Another example from this industry is provided by a Netherlands multinational enterprise which produces specialized products in the Netherlands and the rest of Europe, and complementary consumer products in the United States. Additionally, reference can be made to the Netherlands as a centre of competence in the areas of seed technology, the yeast industry and the gluconate industry, where take-overs by or cooperative ventures with the oil and chemical industries are the rule rather than the exception. Another example is floriculture, where international operations are still restricted to trade, but where direct investment is a definite possibility for the future. Not only are flowers bought from major competitor countries, such as Colombia and Israel, and auctioned on the Netherlands market considering the favourable price and selling climate. Netherlands growers also work together with these competitors in joint attempts to capture the US market, offering a varied supply of flowers throughout the year.[55]

Although it is not possible to generalize in this area, it could well be that this tendency towards product specialization in manufacture and towards *intra*-industry trade will persist. This will definitely be so if, for reasons of cost, the multinational enterprises would tend to diversify to a lesser extent than in the past.[56]

---

[53] Het Economisch Dagblad, December 10, 1982.

[54] De Volkskrant, September 10, 1984.

[55] De Financiële Telegraaf, December 8, 1984; Intermagazine, nr. 11, November 1985, pp. 22-23.

[56] Stopford and Dunning, *op. cit.*, p. 92. Additionally, an important example of a development counter to the 'withdrawal to the own product range' is provided by the drive of the US computer industry to evolve into a full-fledged information industry, leading to acquisitions in the telecommunication industry. Cf. Intermediair 34, August 23, 1985.

Although the services sector is not yet marked by the same degree of international specialization and diversification as the production industries, it may be expected that these tendencies will become increasingly evident in this sector as well – they are, for that matter, already apparent in such sub-sectors as trade, transport and banking and insurance.

In summary, it may be concluded that the trade and investment relations of the open Netherlands economy have acquired a very high international content. These relations would appear to be marked by complementarity to the domestic economy rather than by substitution effects between investment at home and abroad.

7.3 Employment

As noted by Stopford and Dunning, it is tempting to argue that cross-border direct investment entails exporting production capacity and jobs. However, on the basis of the statistics available for various countries, they hold that generally this is not true.[57] According to them, this is due primarily to the fact that an important part of direct investment abroad – probably 50% – concerns operations not having a domestic equivalent, or is undertaken in countries where the enterprise cannot effectively compete from its home base. They note as the second reason that, even if comparable operations are involved, exporting is not always an alternative to direct investment, especially if direct investment serves to evade import curbs or if the foreign market is characterized by very heavy local competition. Thirdly, they hold that, even if jobs are lost in industries which undertake direct investment abroad, such investment generates purchasing power in the recipient country, which may find its way to the country of the direct investor. More in general, Stopford and Dunning note with regard to this subject that the sole adequate response to a lessening of the location advantages of the home base (for instance as a result of relative cost increases) is an improvement in the profitability of the home market. Finally, they point out that outward direct investment constitutes only part of the picture. Other aspects are inward direct investment and the level of economic activity. An increase in cross-border direct investment as a result of, for instance, the exploitation of ownership advantages may cause enterprises abroad to (be forced to) concentrate on and specialize in their own advantages. In turn, they may thus increasingly undertake direct investment in other countries. In this context, Stopford and Dunning give the example of intra-European direct investment which, with increasing European integration, has led to increased product and process specialization of both inward and outward investment. Compare also Pelkmans, who holds that the formation of the EC has led to an increase in prosperity as a consequence of enhanced technical efficiency achieved especially by the multinational enterprises.[58]

[57] Stopford and Dunning, *op. cit.*, pp. 75 ff.

[58] J. Pelkmans, *Market integration in the European Community*, The Hague, 1984.

Table 20
Employment in the Netherlands provided by a number of Netherlands and foreign multinational enterprises

Sector	Number of employees (thousands)			% of total employment		
	1970	1975	1980	1970	1975	1980
Netherlands multinationals						
1 Production industries, mining	292.3	355.1	341.9	25.1	34.0	35.9
2 Retail trade, tourism	–	0.8	53.8	–	0.1	7.5
3 Construction	27.2	42.7	46.8	6.2	11.2	11.7
4 Transport, communication	31.7	31.2	32.6	11.5	11.1	11.1
5 Other services, finance, international trade	67.1	68.7	106.9	9.5	8.2	11.0
6 Total market sector	418.3	498.5	582.0	12.4	15.0	16.9
Foreign multinationals						
1 Production industries, mining	44.5	58.3	115.4	3.9	5.6	12.1
2 Retail trade, tourism	–	1.9	5.8	–	0.3	0.8
3 Construction	–	4.9	3.5	–	1.3	0.9
4 Transport, communication	–	0.6	2.1	–	0.2	0.7
5 Other services, finance, international trade	4.5	14.0	15.5	0.6	1.7	1.6
6 Total market sector	49.0	79.7	142.3	1.5	2.4	4.1

Source: De Jong, *op. cit.* The data have been derived from various sources and are not comparable with those given in Table 21.

The direct investment survey discussed in Chapter 3 does not provide any data about the actual development of employment within multinational enterprises in the Netherlands. In fact, the sources of such information are very few. However, Stopford and Dunning give index figures per country of employment at home and abroad for a limited group of enterprises. For the Netherlands, their figures indicate that between 1977 and 1981 total employment provided by the multinational enterprises *decreased,* though at a slower rate than abroad. Additionally, reference may be made to De Jong's research.[59] Out of the 1,000 largest enterprises in the Netherlands in 1980 examined by him, 355 were multinationals, of which 128 were Netherlands-owned and 227 foreign-owned. The development of employment provided in the Netherlands by these Netherlands multinationals is shown in Table 20.

Whereas between 1970 and 1980 employment in the total Netherlands market sector increased barely, the number of jobs provided by the Netherlands multination-

[59] De Jong, *op. cit.*

Table 21
Employment and number of establishments of foreign enterprises in the Netherlands, broken down by period of establishment

Period of establishment	Employment		Number of establishments			
			Total		of which: production industries	
	Abs.	(%)	Abs.	(%)	Abs.	(%)
until 1946	24,306	(21.9)	114	(100.0)	30	(26.3)
1946/1959	23,949	(21.6)	164	(100.0)	62	(37.8)
1960/1974	54,964	(49.6)	686	(100.0)	161	(23.5)
1975/1984	7,661	(6.9)	341	(100.0)	35	(10.3)
Total	110,880	(100.0)	1,305	(100.0)	288	(22.1)

Source: Geographical Institute of the University of Utrecht, 1984. The data have been derived from the university's own sources and are not comparable with those given in Table 20.

als included in De Jong's study went up by nearly 40 %, from 418,300 to 582,000. The share of these multinationals in total employment thus increased from 12.5 % to 17 %. This does not, however, alter the fact that the employment abroad provided by these multinationals developed even more favourably. But, as noted before, no consistent data on this subject are available.[60]

The number of jobs provided in the Netherlands by foreign-owned multinationals nearly tripled to 142,300; however, the share in total employment remained limited to less than 5 %. It is interesting to compare these figures from De Jong's study with those of the Geographical Institute of the University of Utrecht. According to the latter's study, wholly or partly foreign-owned enterprises in the Netherlands employed 203,544 persons in 1984. The breakdown by type of enterprise shows that 110,880 persons were employed by direct establishments of foreign multinationals, 80,885 by Netherlands enterprises taken over by foreign multinationals and 11,779 by joint ventures. Of the total, nearly 60 % was employed in the production industries, nearly 25 % in trade and distribution and the remainder in other services.

Closer examination of employment provided by direct establishments of foreign multinationals shows that 22 % of the total of 110,880 persons were employed by

[60] J.T. de Mare's study indicates an increase in the foreign share in total employment, although this may differ for various types of multinational enterprises. For instance, employment in the Netherlands provided by the most highly multinationalized enterprises (more than 25 % of the total number of employees abroad) increased in the period 1970-1980, while that provided by enterprises where the number of jobs abroad account for 10-25 % of total employment increased between 1970 and 1975 and decreased between 1975 and 1980. However, here too, discrepancies are apparent when Netherlands figures for different periods are compared. Economisch Statistische Berichten, August 28, 1985.

trade and distribution		other services	
Abs.	(%)	Abs.	(%)
65	(57.0)	19	(16.7)
70	(42.7)	32	(19.5)
390	(56.8)	135	(19.7)
220	(64.5)	86	(25.2)
745	(57.1)	272	(20.8)

establishments formed before 1946, a similar percentage by establishments formed in the period 1946-1959 and half by those set up in the years 1960-1974 (Table 21). Employment provided by direct establishment formed after 1974 was markedly less; however, it must be noted that these establishments have had less time to expand and that they may be expected to show a further increase in employment in the years ahead. As in the case of direct investment positions, the number of direct establishments also shows a shift from the production industries towards trade and services (Table 21).

The study also examined the movements in employment provided by these Netherlands establishments of foreign multinational enterprises in the period 1980-1984. Although employment provided by establishments in the production industries decreased by 5 %, this compared very favourably with the development of *total* employment in the production industries, which went down by over 12 %. Furthermore, employment provided by establishments in trade and distribution increased by 7 %, while the number of jobs at establishments in the services sector went up by 2 %. For all sectors combined, 'foreign employment' decreased on balance by 1.5 %; this was entirely due to dismissals and restructuring operations at newly acquired enterprises. However, the number of jobs provided by direct establishments increased on balance, which was largely due to a sharp growth of employment at recent establishments.

The Geographical Institute's study concludes that 'foreign operations in the Netherlands represent a relatively strong element of the Netherlands economy and may hold out important prospects for future developments'.

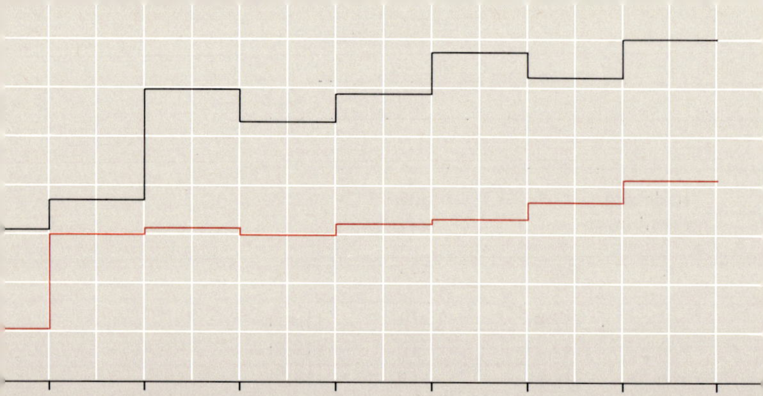

gn direct investment in the Netherlands (B)

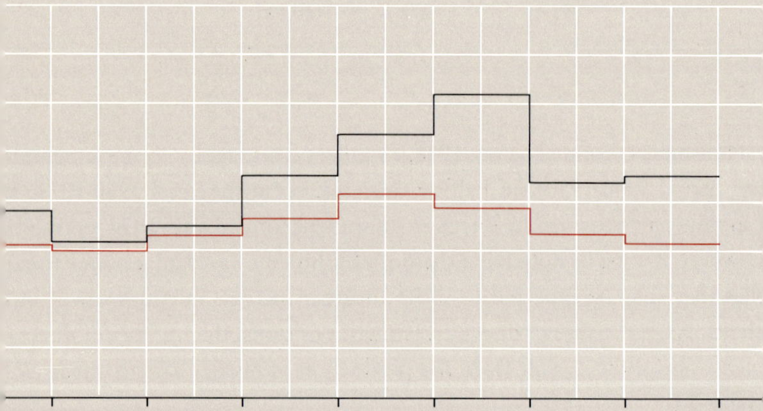

direct investment (A–B)

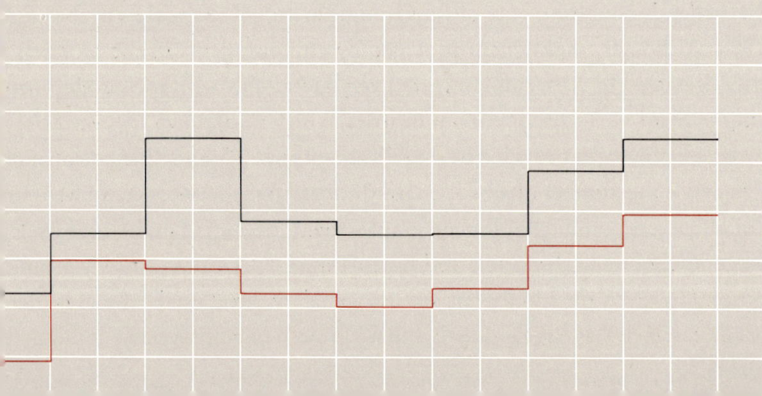

Chart 2
Composition of survey and distribution of participation percentages, 1983

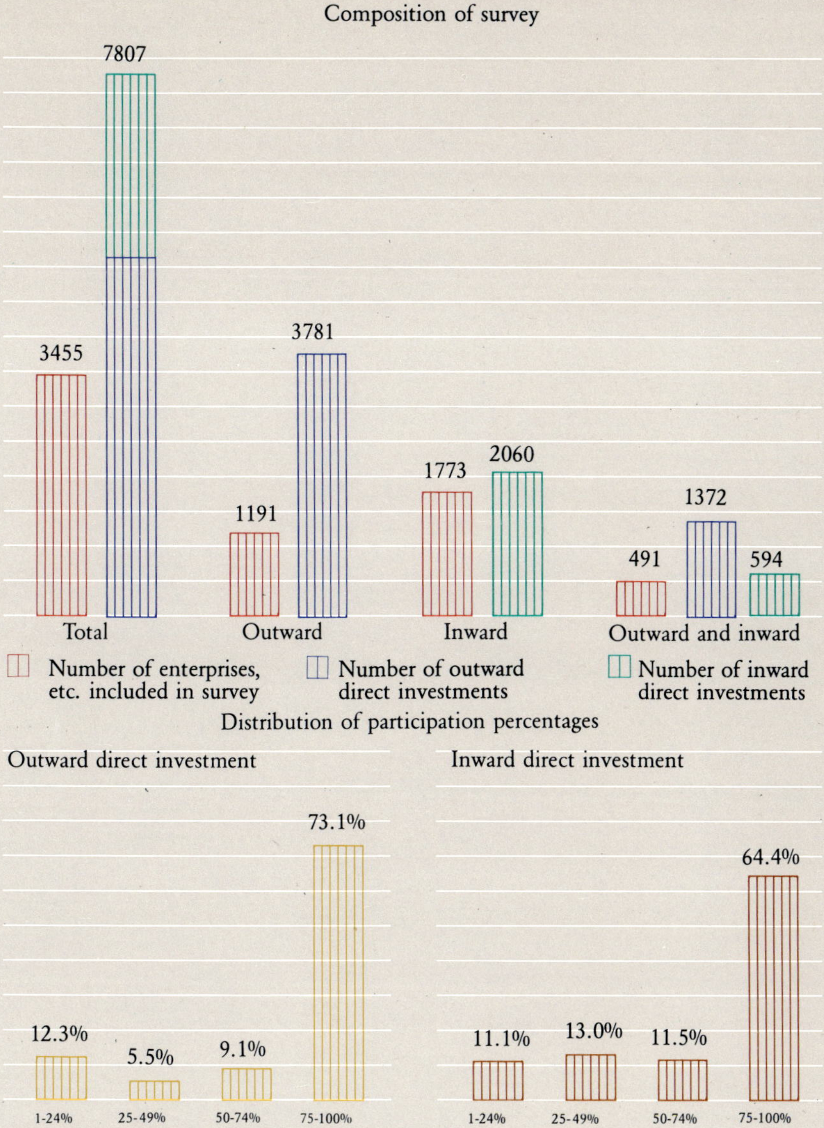

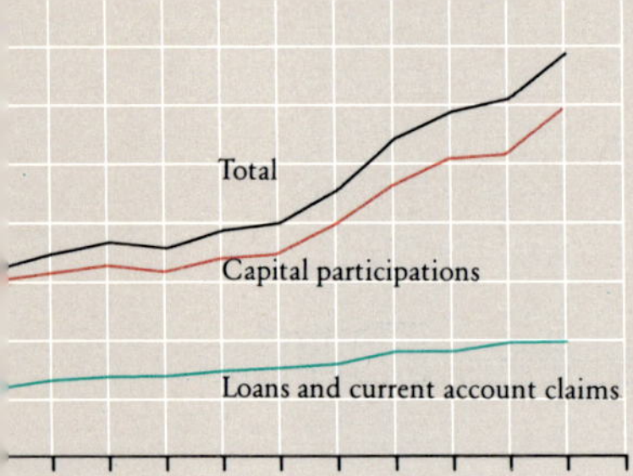

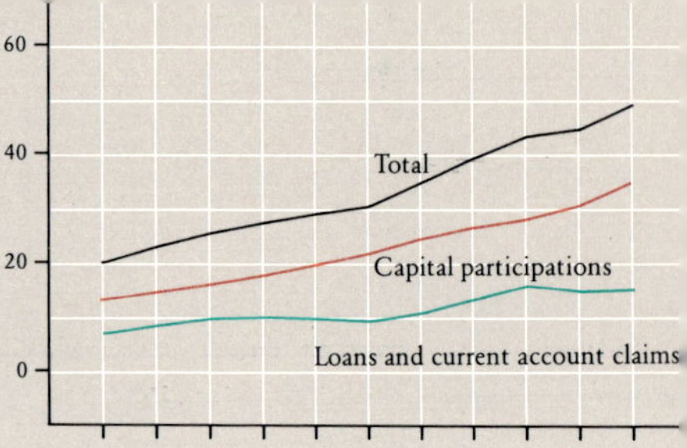

stment income (billions of guilders)

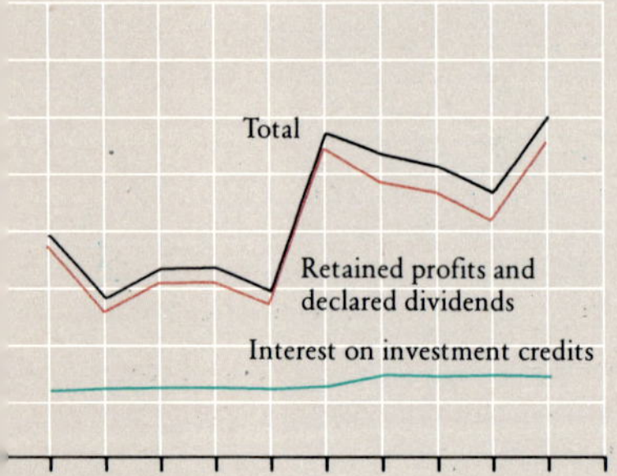

Investment income (billions of guilders)

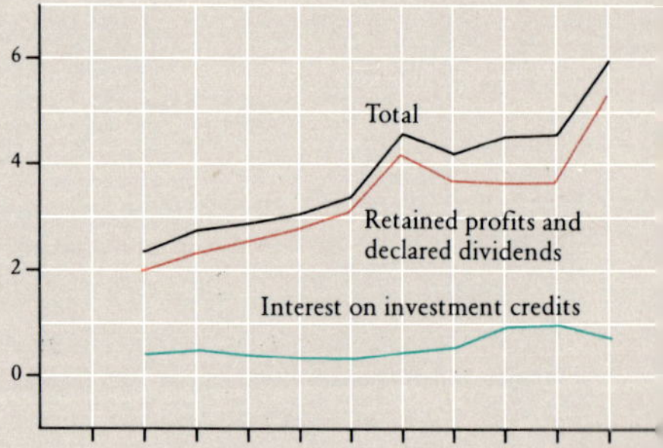

s of return (%)

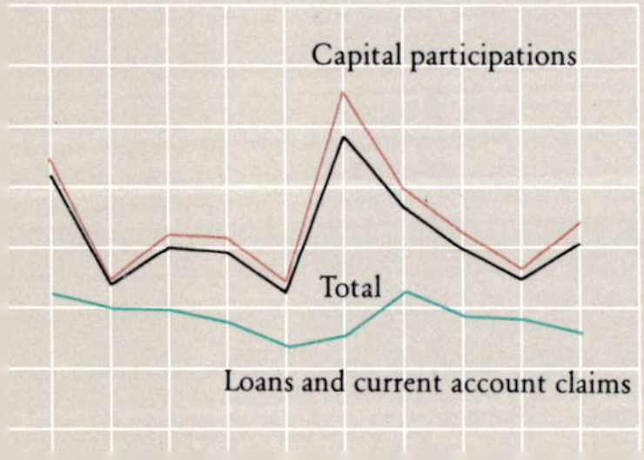

Rates of return (%)

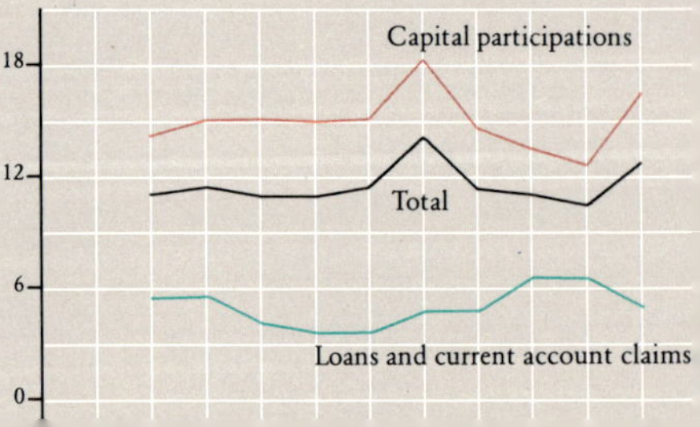

Chart 4
Netherlands direct investment position abroad, broken down by sector

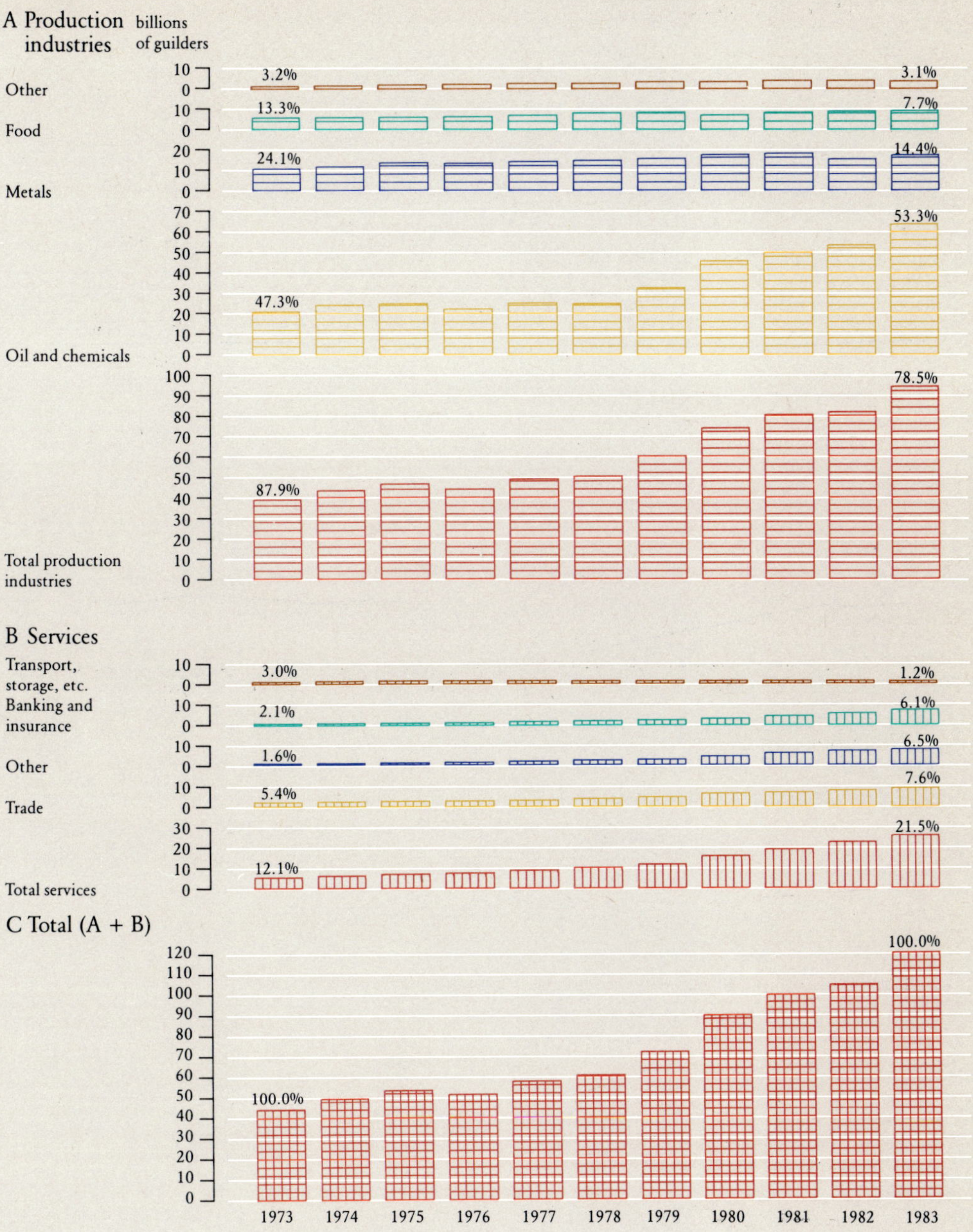

Chart 5
Rates of return on Netherlands direct investment abroad, broken down by sector [1]

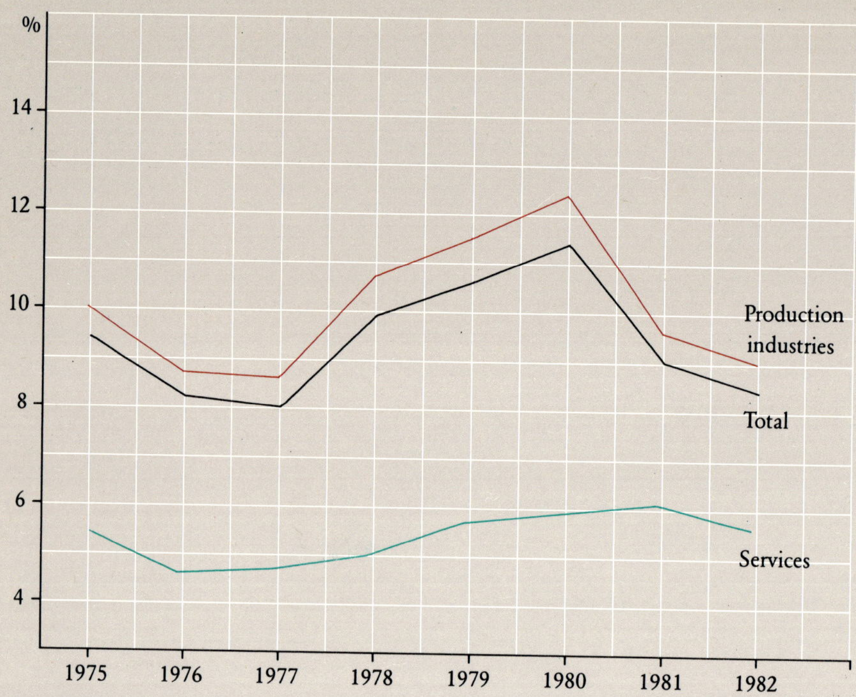

[1] Moving 3-year average.

Chart 6
Foreign direct investment position in the Netherlands, broken down by sector

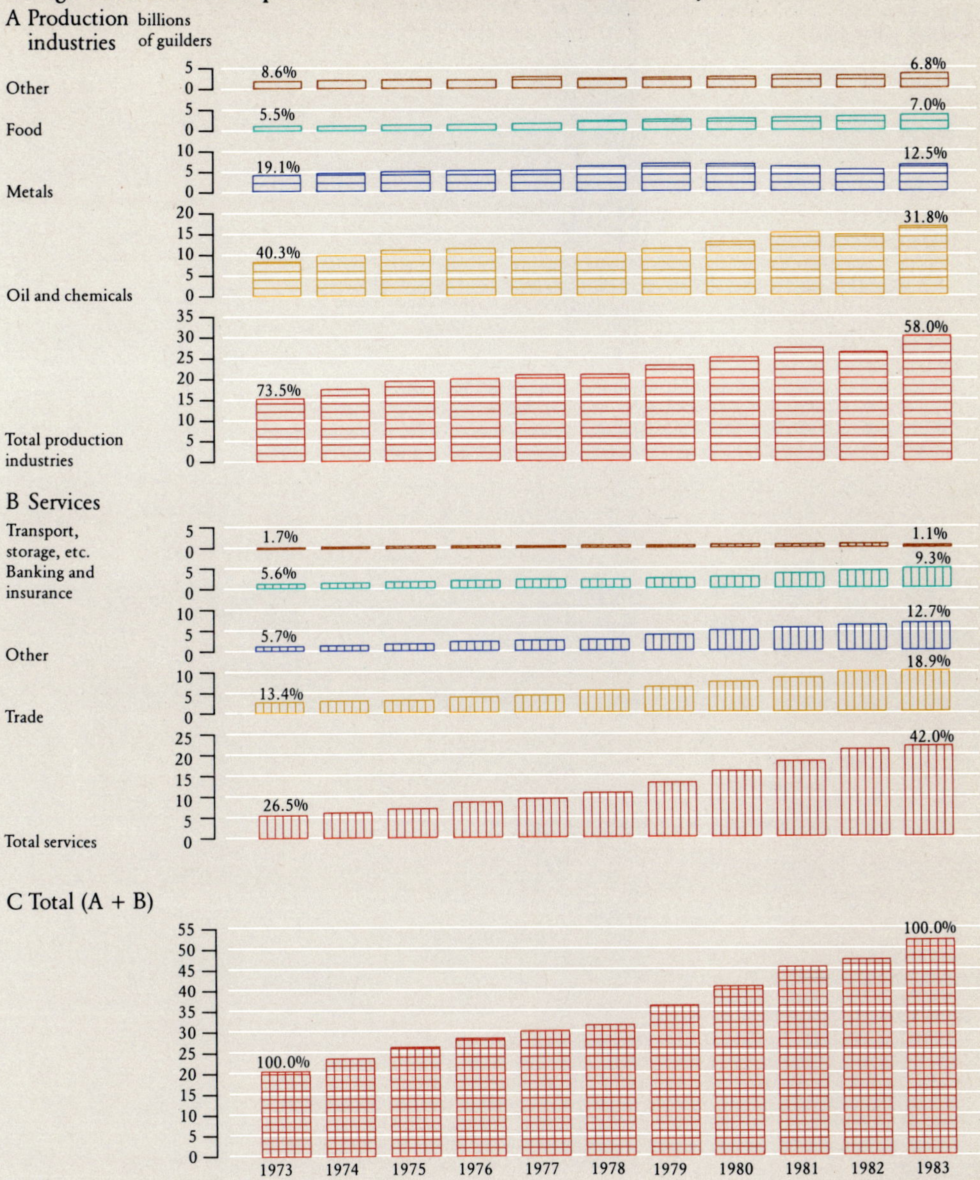

Chart 7
Rates of return on foreign direct investment in the Netherlands, broken down by sector [1]

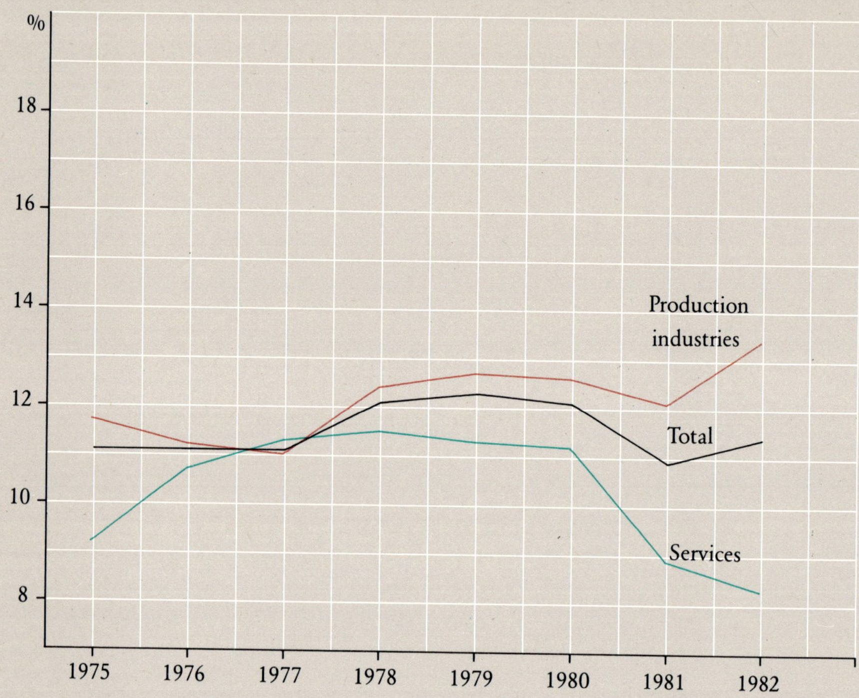

[1] Moving 3-year average.

Chart 8
Net direct investment position of the Netherlands, broken down by sector

Chart 9
Netherlands direct investment position abroad, broken down by country

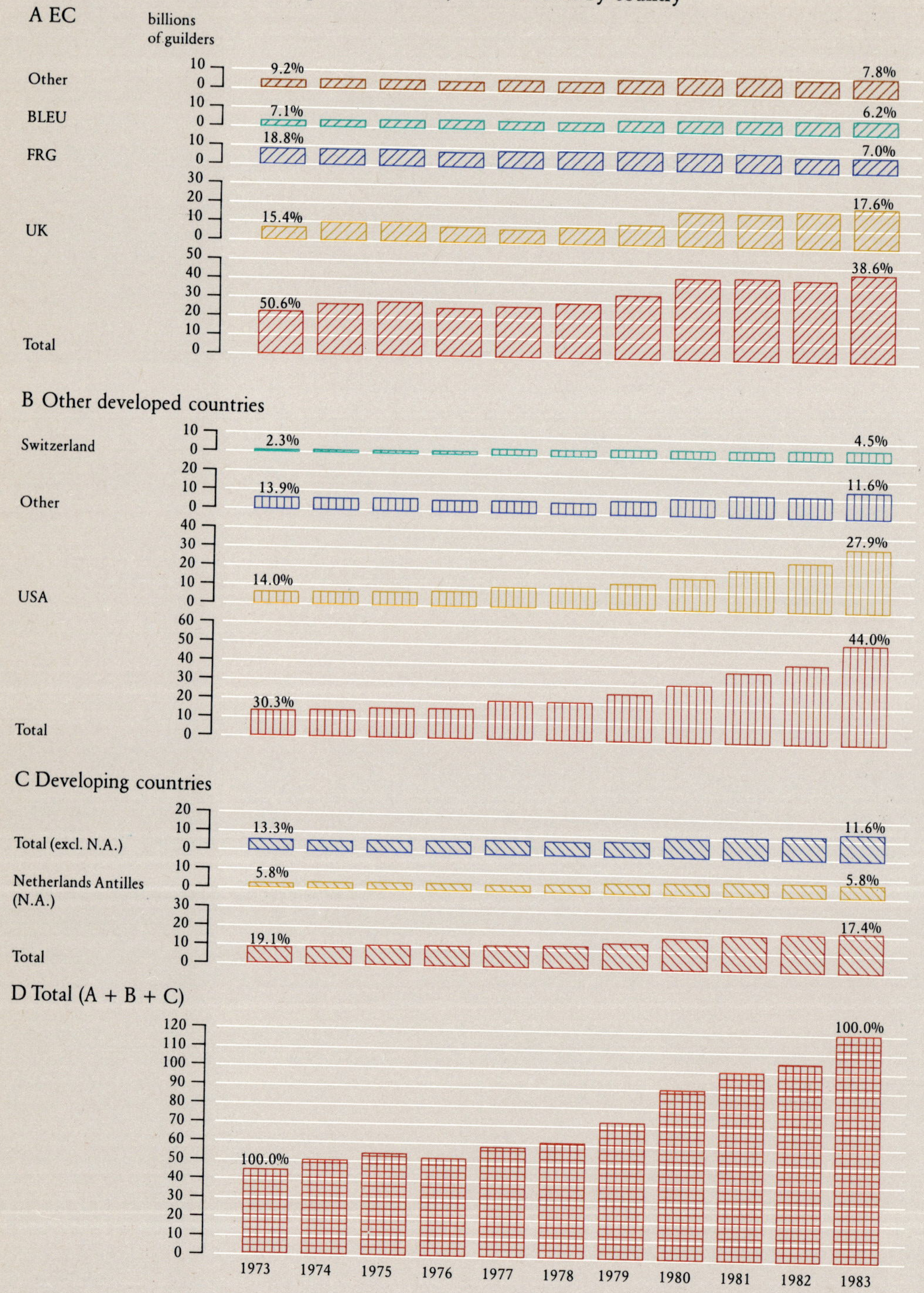

Chart 10
Rates of return on Netherlands direct investment abroad, broken down by country [1]

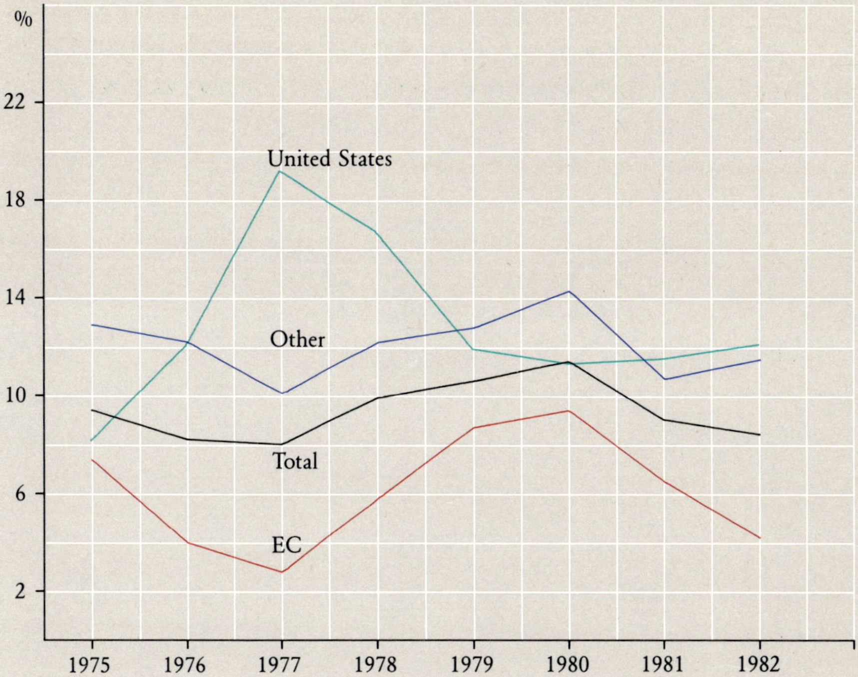

[1] Moving 3-year average.

Chart 11
Foreign direct investment position in the Netherlands, broken down by country

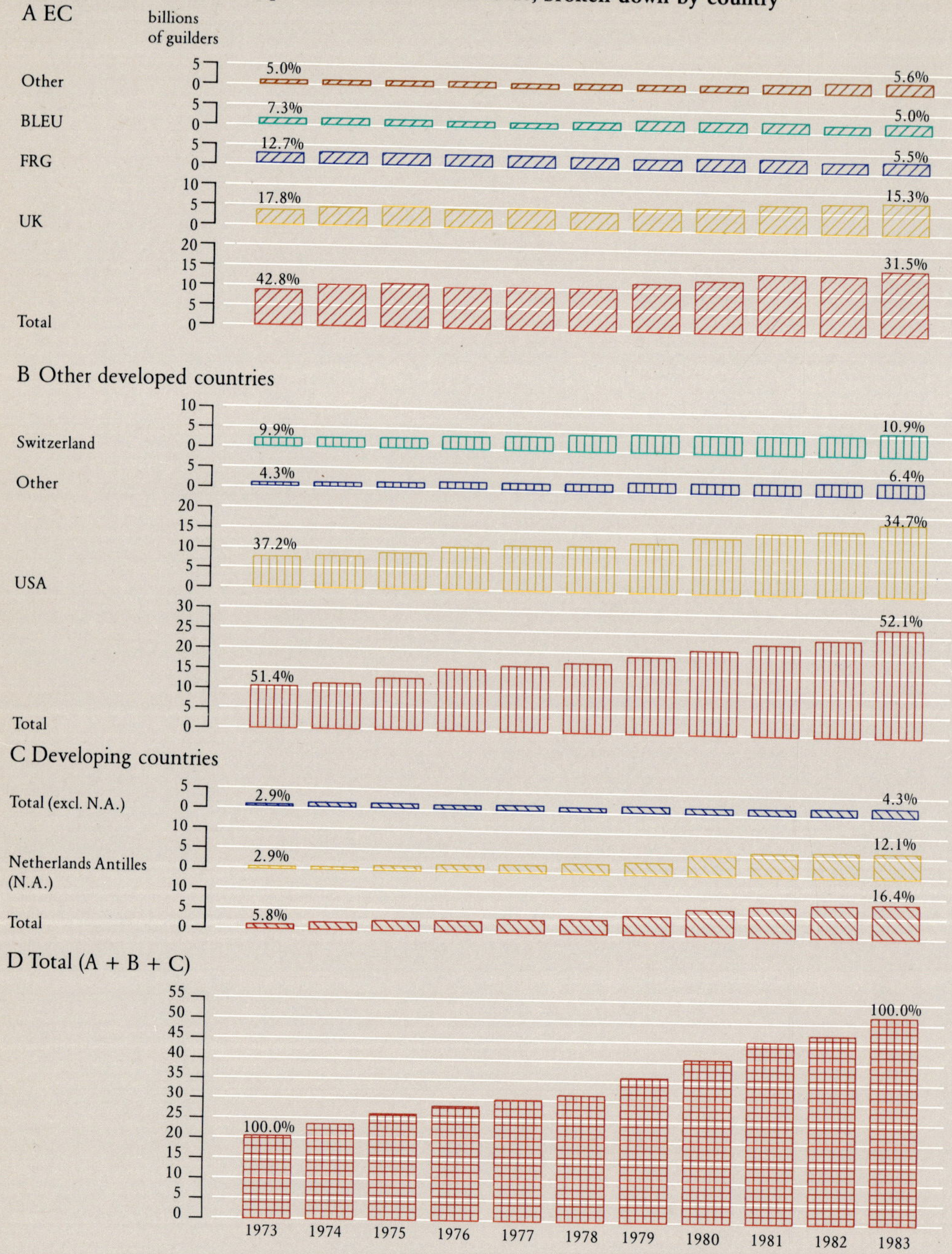

Chart 12
Direct establishments of foreign enterprises in the Netherlands during four periods, broken down by nationality

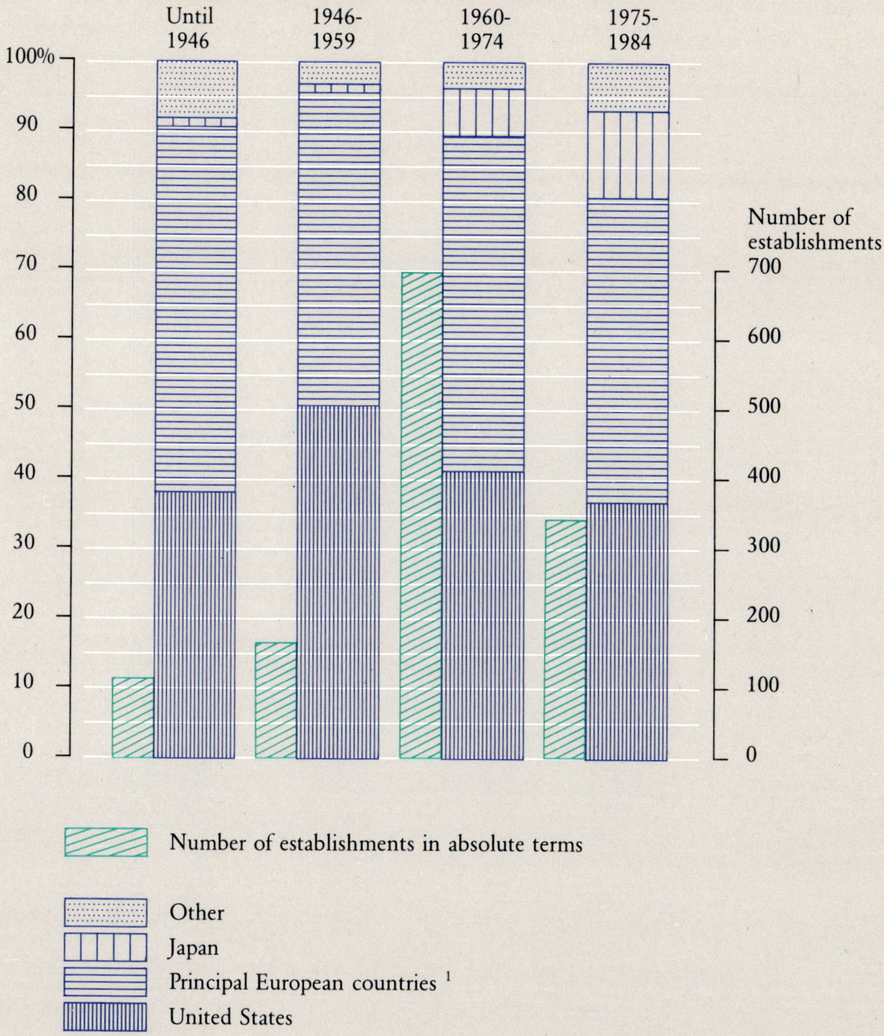

[1] Federal Republic of Germany, France, United Kingdom, Sweden and Switzerland.

Source: Geographical Institute of the University of Utrecht, 1984.

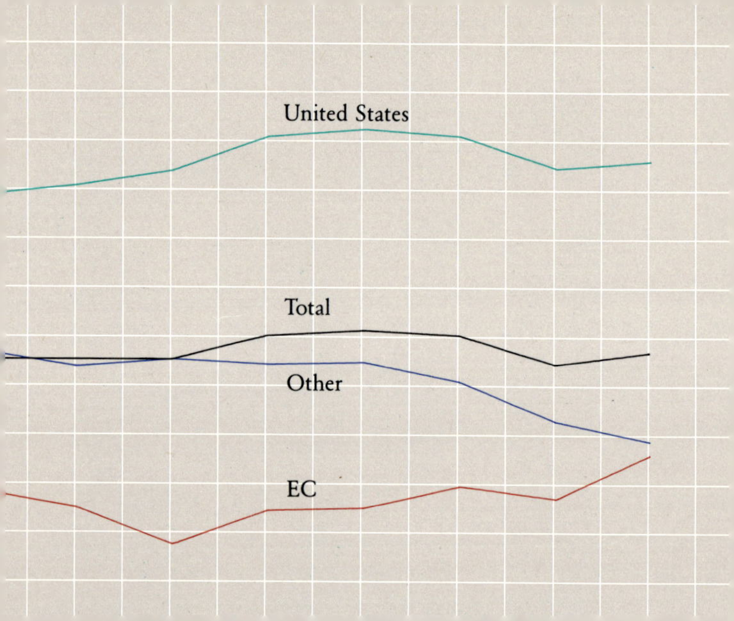
United States
Total
Other
EC

Chart 14
Net direct investment position of the Netherlands, broken down by country

Chart 15
Netherlands direct investment position abroad at the end of 1973, 1978, 1982 and 1983
(billions of guilders and % of grand total per annum)

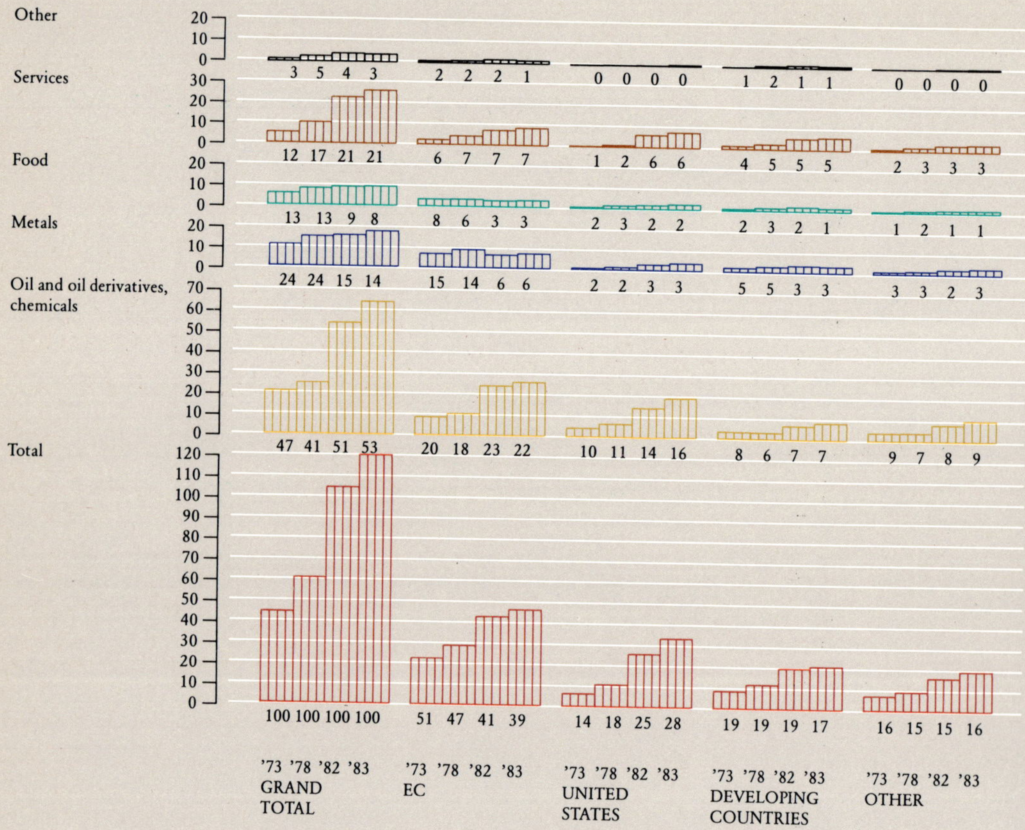

Chart 16
Direct investment, broken down by sector and by country
(% of total)

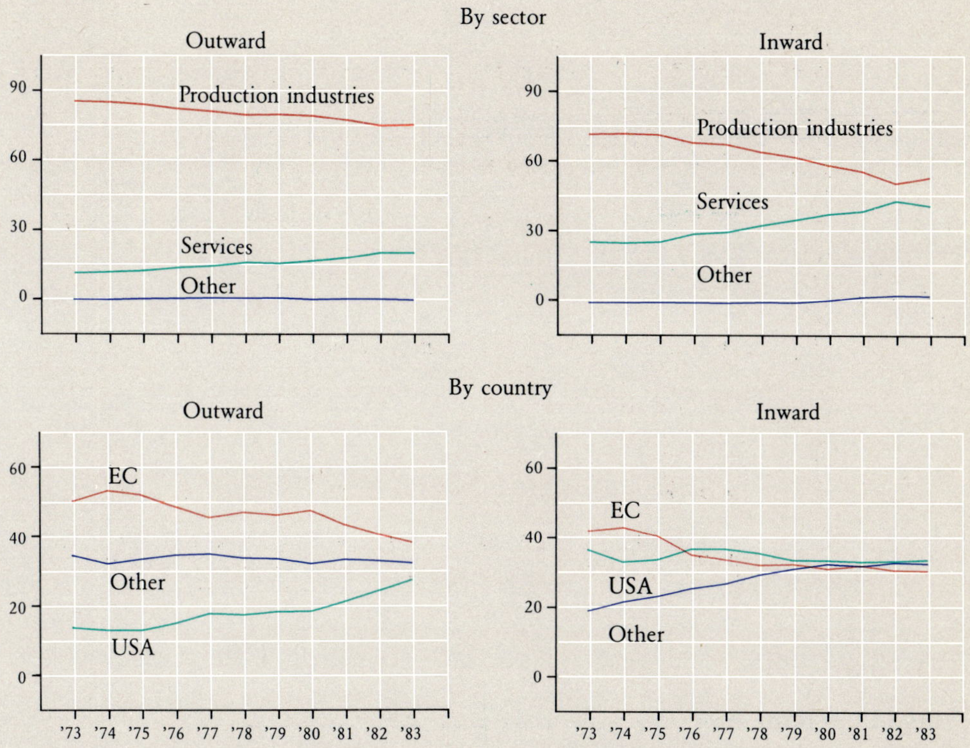

Chart 17
Foreign direct investment position in the Netherlands at the end of 1973, 1978, 1982 and 1983
(billions of guilders and % of grand total per annum)

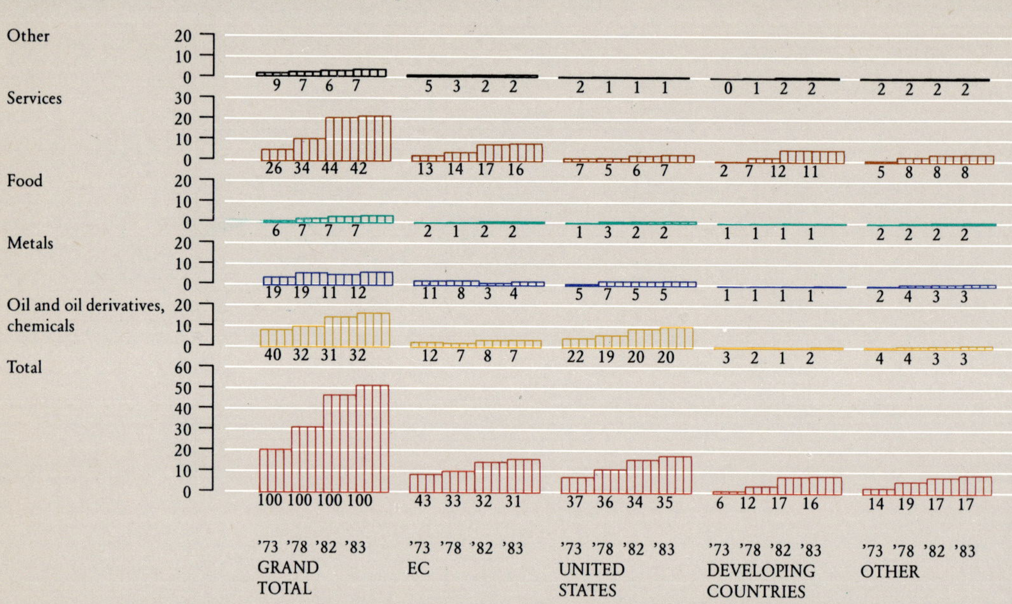

Appendix A: Netherlands statistical methodology for direct investment

1 The concept of cross-border direct investment

1.1 IMF and OECD definitions

For various historical and practical reasons, direct investment is not defined uniformly in all countries. In order to improve the international comparability of statistics, international organizations, notably the IMF and the OECD, have attempted to come to a uniform delimitation.

According to the IMF, direct investment refers to investment that is made to acquire a *lasting* interest in an enterprise operating in an economy other than that of the investor, the investor's purpose being to have an *effective* voice in the management of the enterprise.[1]

As this definition still left too much scope for individual interpretation, attempts were made within the OECD to come to such an elaboration that the resulting definition would be practicable for all countries, regardless of their manner of compiling statistics. In 1983 this led to a 'Detailed Benchmark Definition on Foreign Direct Investment', containing detailed recommendations regarding all sorts of registration problems pertaining to this subject. This methodology aims at providing a standard to which the individual countries should suit their systems gradually in the course of time. According to the Benchmark Definition, a direct investment relationship is marked by:

- voting power or a shareholding of 10 % or over, unless it can be established that this does not allow any effective voice in the management, or
- voting power or a shareholding of less than 10 % (or none) but an effective voice in the management.

Consequently, the basic criterion is an effective voice in the management; in principle, the shareholding percentage, which was initially the primary factor in the deliberations leading to the definition, is not relevant.

1.2 Practice in the Netherlands

The delimitation of the concept of direct investment used in the Netherlands meets the criterion that direct investment is characterized by the acquisition of a more or less lasting interest in an enterprise, with the aim of having an effective voice in the management. In practice, the condition applies that this must be attended by a shareholding, irrespective of its percentage.

Purchases on the stock exchange are always classified as portfolio investment (security transactions). In the event that such purchases should lead in time to an actual direct investment relationship, intra-group transfers, etc. will often ensue,

---

[1] Balance of Payments Manual, 4th edition, 1977, paragraph 408.

which will be recognized as such in the balance-of-payments registration. Hence, the direct investment relationship will become evident later. If residents sell or buy shareholdings direct, i.e. not on the stock exchange, the resident concerned is requested to state the nature of the transaction (portfolio investment or direct investment). Finally, information is obtained from annual reports and publications in the media.

2 Manner of collecting data

In a number of countries, including the Netherlands and France, transaction data about direct investment are primarily collected within the framework of the balance-of-payments registration; this registration is monolithic in nature in that each payment is recorded within a single uniform framework ('exchange control registration'). Moreover, since 1973 the Netherlands has also collected data by means of annual surveys of the positions of outward and inward direct investment.

2.1 Balance-of-payments data

The direct investment data included in the balance of payments relate to the direct investment flows between residents and non-residents. *Capital participations* are generally acquired by direct purchases of shares. However, capital participations can also be acquired without any payment, for instance by an exchange of shares or by the acquisition of shares against the transfer of claims, goods, licences or know-how. All these transactions are recorded in the statistics concerned. In addition to capital participations, the direct investment registration includes – in conformity with the IMF and OECD guidelines – all short and long-term intra-group *lending* and all intra-group *current accounts.*

The balance-of-payments data are published in the Bank's Annual Reports and Quarterly Bulletins, about two or three months after the period of registration.

2.2 Survey data

The position figures, which are compiled by means of the annual surveys, may change as a result of the following factors:

a. Changes ensuing from changes in capital participations and/or in intra-group lending positions. These are the *capital flows.* They may be due to such transactions as purchases or sales of shares and the granting or repayment of intra-group credits and loans.
b. Changes ensuing from the retention of *profits* or the absorption of losses by subsidiaries.
c. Changes ensuing from *exchange rate differences,* other revaluations and adjustments.

As the Netherlands balance of payments includes only the capital flows under a. above, the changes in positions are more comprehensive than the changes in direct investment shown in the balance of payments; cases in point are retained profits, exchange rate differences and revaluations (see also Chapter 4 and Appendix B).

Appendix B: Retained profits and the balance of payments

1 Introduction

The internationally agreed methods for accounting for retained profits of foreign subsidiaries are not uniform where the balance of payments and the National Accounts are concerned. The third edition of the International Monetary Fund's Balance of Payments Manual, which was published in 1961, already recommended that retained profits be included in the balance of payments together with distributed profits. This investment income item in the current account would have to be offset by a direct investment item in the capital account. In the fourth edition of the Manual (1977) this recommendation was maintained. However, up to now it has *not* been taken over in the System of National Accounts of the United Nations, so that retained profits are not included in the rest of the world accounts of the National Accounts.

2 Arguments in favour of inclusion in the System of National Accounts

The following arguments are advanced *in favour of* including retained profits in the balance of payments and the National Accounts:

a. Generally, a direct investor has power to decide on the profit distribution policy of the direct investment enterprise. A decision to retain profits may thus be seen as a deliberate choice of the direct investor to increase his interest at the sacrifice of the income due to him.
b. Differences in profit distribution policies among countries (owing to government regulations, etc.) and among enterprises may thus be eliminated in the balance of payments.
c. In many countries direct investment income has both economic and political significance and it is considered useful to reflect total earned income in the statistics for the calculation of return on direct investment.
d. Retained profits increase the direct investment position, and inclusion of such profits in the balance of payments means the visualization of the 'investments' involved (contra entry in capital account) and, hence, of the change in the international financial relationship.

3 Arguments against inclusion

The following arguments are advanced *against* inclusion:

a. Profits retained by foreign subsidiaries are to be viewed as investments of the subsidiary rather than the parent. They are in fact generated from the subsidiary's savings and must therefore be allocated to the economy of the country in which the subsidiary is located.
b. In countries compiling only a balance of payments on a cash basis, retained profits are not recorded since they are not actually transferred.

c. It is not meaningful to inflate the national income of a country which happens to accommodate the holding company of a multinational group by adding the retained profits of subsidiaries.

4 Practice in the Netherlands

In the Netherlands, retained profits are still published separately and are not included in the balance of payments. This is due to the fact that the cons of inclusion are held to carry more weight than the pros. Moreover, this procedure ensures consistency of the balance of payments and the National Accounts. In this respect, a role is also played by the fact that data about retained profits can only be obtained *after* the closing of the financial year by the enterprises concerned by means of enquiries. Hence, in practice this means that data about retained profits only become available long after publication of the balance of payments.

Appendix C: Discrepancies between Netherlands and US statistics

There are major discrepancies between Netherlands and US statistics on the bilateral direct investment positions. According to the most recent Benchmark Survey – for 1980 – of the US Department of Commerce (Bureau of Economic Analysis), the Netherlands direct investment position in the United States totals \$ 19,354 million or, converted into 1980 guilders, Fl. 41,214 million. Thus, according to the US registration, the Netherlands ranks first among the foreign investors in the United States, ahead of such countries as the United Kingdom and Canada. This figure of Fl. 41.2 billion for 1980 contrasts sharply with that of Fl. 16.9 billion which can be derived from the Netherlands statistics on direct investment positions. This discrepancy is due to various causes, which are discussed below (in order of decreasing importance).

1. The US balance-of-payments statistics employ different classification criteria. The principal criterion is that of the direct relationship with *'each member of the Foreign Parent Group* (FPG)', irrespective of majority or minority interest. This relationship governs the geographical classification in the statistics on direct investment positions or in the balance of payments. In principle, this does not differ from the method used in the Netherlands. However, in the US statistics all direct investment from the Netherlands to the United States is allocated to the Netherlands, including that of foreign groups' intermediate holding companies in the Netherlands. However, in the Netherlands statistics this direct investment by such intermediate holding companies or 'Special Financial Institutions' (SFIs), as they are called in the Netherlands, is recorded separately (see Appendix D: Special Financial Institutions).

   Some indication of the importance of this difference may be afforded by applying another criterion used in the above-mentioned US statistics: the *'Ultimate Beneficial Owner* (UBO)' criterion. Under this criterion, classification is solely by the ultimate owner having the largest interest. However, even though the use of this criterion does indeed ensure the elimination of direct investment by SFIs it does the same for direct investment in the United States by foreign companies' subsidiaries long rooted in the Netherlands. In the Netherlands statistics, however, direct investment by these often very independent subsidiaries, most of whose operations are closely integrated in the Netherlands economy, are classified as *Netherlands* outward direct investment. Consequently, the shift from the FPG to the UBO criterion results in some 'overadjustment'. The differences shown in Table C1 are thus unduly large.

   For 1980, the Netherlands direct investment position in the United States according to the UBO criterion proves to be nearly *one-half* (\$ 10 billion) of that measured by the FPG criterion.

   After adjustment for the intermediate holding companies, etc., the Netherlands direct investment position in the United States should *at the very least* be: \$ 10.6 billion x 2.1295 = Fl. 22.6 billion. This is still higher than the amount of

Table C1
Direct investment positions in the United States in 1980, measured by various US classification criteria

(millions of dollars)	By country of each member of the foreign parent group (FPG)		By country of Ultimate Beneficial Owner (UBO)		Differences (FPG and UBO)	
	Foreign direct invest-ment position in the US	Direct invest-ment income	Foreign direct invest-ment position in the US	Direct invest-ment income	Foreign direct invest-ment position in the US	Direct invest-ment income
Netherlands	19,354	3,231	10,599	1,268	8,755	1,963
United Kingdom	13,684	1,173	17,236	2,480	-3,552	-1,307
Canada	10,786	600	13,846	1,067	-3,060	-467
Germany	7,450	-106	9,128	-8	-1,678	-98
Switzerland	5,034	215	6,173	314	-1,139	-99
France	3,637	242	5,531	302	-1,894	-60
Japan	4,264	682	4,345	676	-81	6
Latin America	9,027	821	2,645	456	6,382	365
Rest of the world	6,714	374	10,447	677	-3,733	-303
All countries	79,950	7,232	79,950	7,232	-	-

Source: Foreign direct investment in the United States, 1980. US-Department of Commerce (BEA), Table 9.

Fl. 16.9 billion according to the Netherlands statistics. The discrepancy is accounted for by a number of other factors.

2. Another major cause is the fact that, if a subsidiary in the United States is owned by a foreign transnational group whose holding company is established in more than one country, the US statistics allocate the direct investment in this subsidiary wholly to the country having the largest direct interest. In practice, this causes the US statistics to show a higher amount of Netherlands direct investment than the Netherlands statistics. This factor is very roughly estimated to account for a difference of over Fl. 7 billion.
3. Additionally, the US statistics consistently classify investment in real estate as direct investment. An exception is made for second homes for personal use. In the Netherlands statistics, investment in real estate is, in principle, classified as portfolio investment, except for purchases of industrial sites and buildings by property companies for business purposes. According to Netherlands balance-of-payments data, this involved an amount of accumulated portfolio investment flows to the United States of Fl. 1.5 billion in the period 1970-1980.

4. A further source of discrepancies is the fact that the US Department of Commerce classifies any acquisition by a non-resident of more than 10% of the share capital of an US company as direct investment, irrespective of whether the shareholding is used to exert influence on that company's management. In the Netherlands balance of payments (in conformity with the guidelines of the International Monetary Fund), acquisition of shares in a foreign company is classified as direct investment only if this is attended by actual and lasting influence on the company's management. Transactions not meeting this criterion (such as investment transactions by security or property investment companies) are classified as portfolio investment in the Netherlands balance of payments. The consequent differences are not known, but are not likely to be very large, possibly Fl. 0.5 billion at most.
5. The scope of the US statistics on direct investment positions is broader. Contrary to the Netherlands statistics, they include data regarding foreign-owned unincorporated branches, sales offices, etc. The amount involved is presumably not very large, possibly Fl. 0.5 billion at most.
6. In the US statistics, the intra-group relationship governs the classification of capital transactions into domestic and foreign capital. In this system, international intra-group loans granted by subsidiaries to, for instance, parent companies are regarded as disinvestments by the latter. In the Netherlands statistics, such loans, with the exception of intra-group current accounts, are classified as outward direct investment by the subsidiary. However, this factor would not appear to be a major source of discrepancies either.

If the differences arising from the causes listed above under 2 to 5 are added to the amounts according to the Netherlands statistics, Netherlands direct investment in the United States would very roughly come out at Fl. 16.9 billion + Fl. 9.5 billion = Fl. 26.4 billion or $ 12.4 billion. This is some $ 2 billion higher than the UBO position; this is due in part to the fact that the latter does not include foreign-owned subsidiaries in the Netherlands which engage in actual economic activity and also make investments in the United States.

Regarding the actual direct investment position in the United States, the Netherlands figures would appear to reflect to a greater extent the direct investors' significance to the Netherlands economy. The Netherlands figures show, as it were, the structural relationship between the Netherlands and US economies through the direct investment position. The US figures would appear to stress the direct transaction principle (FPG criterion), on the one hand, and the purely legal relationships (UBO criterion), on the other.

If investing countries are to be *ranked* in terms of their direct investment positions in the United States, it is essential that one and the same (US) source be used, as it is not known to what extent the differences listed above also apply in respect of other countries. On the basis of the UBO criterion, the Netherlands would be the *third* largest investor in the United States, a position which the Netherlands had, incidentally, already reached in the 1930s.

Appendix D: Special Financial Institutions (SFIs)

1. Ever since the early 1970s, an increasing number of Special Financial Institutions (SFIs) has been established in the Netherlands. SFIs are resident enterprises and institutions, irrespective of their legal form, in which non-residents are directly or indirectly participating by means of share capital or otherwise and which have as their object or make it largely their business to receive funds from non-residents and to pass on these funds to non-residents.

   In practice, SFIs are notably foreign companies' subsidiaries in the Netherlands which channel payments via the Netherlands, such as holding and finance companies, royalty and motion picture companies, reinvoicing companies, factoring companies, distribution companies and (in recent years) foreign sales corporations. Mixtures of these forms also occur frequently.
2. The reasons underlying establishment in the Netherlands are basically the openness of the economy and the attractive economic climate, the freedom of capital movements, the high legal security and the political stability, and the attractive tax climate for internationally operating companies.
3. In line with the treatment of goods merchanting transactions by Netherlands merchants, which are recorded in a separate balance-of-payments category (as net merchanting under services, instead of mixed up with goods transactions), observed transactions by SFIs are shown net in a separate balance-of-payments category. For 1983 and 1984, the net amounts shown in Table D1 were recorded under 'Other long-term foreign capital'.

   In 1983 a net inflow of Fl. 0.9 billion was recorded. This may have been due to both actual portfolio investment, direct investment or other activities of SFIs in the Netherlands and to statistical factors (items in transit, etc.). In 1984, on the other hand, the SFI flows led to an aggregate net outflow of Fl. 0.5 billion.
4. The net inflow in 1983 of Fl. 0.9 billion and the net outflow in 1984 of Fl. 0.5 billion are made up of considerable gross flows. For international comparisons of balance-of-payments statistics, it may be desirable to take these gross flows into account as well (cf. Appendix C). A further breakdown of the net amounts into current and capital transactions shows that in 1983 about Fl. 23 billion in current transactions and Fl. 44.5 billion in capital transactions were channelled via Netherlands SFIs (Table D2). In 1984 the capital transactions had increased to Fl. 66-68 billion.

   The *current* transactions show the diversity of the SFI flows. The visible transactions are largely accounted for by the leasing companies, distribution centres, etc. The item services comprises bank charges, issuing costs, overheads, etc. The interest and dividend payments included in factor income are accounted for by the finance and holding companies, and the royalties and motion picture rights by the companies acquiring (sub)licences in respect of patents and movie rights. Overlaps and mixtures with operations in the Netherlands are increasingly evident.

Table D1
Net SFI flows shown in the Netherlands balance of payments
(billions of guilders)

	1983	1984
Total	0.9	-0.5

Table D2
Breakdown of SFI transactions
(billions of guilders)

Description	1983			1984		
	receipts	payments	net	receipts	payments	net
1 Current transactions	22.9	21.8	1.1	21.2	24.2	-3.0
of which: goods	(11.2)	(11.6)	(-0.4)	(8.9)	(8.1)	(0.8)
services	(0.8)	(1.2)	(-0.4)	(1.0)	(1.2)	(-0.2)
factor income	(10.9)	(9.0)	(1.9)	(11.3)	(14.9)	(-3.6)
2 Capital transactions	44.4	44.6	-0.2	68.3	65.8	2.5
Total (1 + 2)	67.3	66.4	0.9	89.5	90.0	-0.5

Table D3
Results of SFI survey on assets and liabilities, as at end-1983
(billions of guilders)

Foreign assets		*Foreign liabilities*	
1 Participations	54.1	1 Capital and reserves	45.5
2 Intra-group loans [1]	65.0	2 Intra-group loans	47.4
3 Intra-group current accounts	7.4	3 Intra-group current accounts	10.0
4 Total investment by SFIs	126.5	4 Total investment in SFIs	102.9
5 Other loans	11.3	5 Bonds and notes	34.2
6 Time deposits and bank balances	4.0	6 Bank loans	9.9
7 Other assets [2]	13.1	7 Other liabilities	7.9
	154.9		154.9

[1] Including bonds issued by affiliated companies.
[2] Including a small amount relating to net domestic assets and statistical discrepancies.

Contrary to the net amounts given in Table D1, the gross changes shown in Table D2 are not entered as such in the Netherlands balance of payments, that is, not in the relevant categories mixed up with the transactions of non-SFIs.

5. A good impression of the capital transactions of the SFIs is afforded by annual surveys. See the overview of the *positions* of the assets and liabilities of the SFIs as at end-1983 (Table D3).

Of the balance sheet total of Fl. 155 billion, nearly two-thirds had been financed from intra-group funds. Additionally, Fl. 34 billion had been raised through bond and note issues and Fl. 10 billion in the form of bank loans.

It must be noted that, apart from statistical discrepancies, the item 'Other assets' also includes domestic assets and liabilities still to be classified. To the extent that it has meanwhile proved possible to classify these items, they have been registered elsewhere in the Netherlands balance of payments. At the end of 1983 this concerned an accumulated amount of over Fl. 200 million of mainly direct investment in the Netherlands. Additionally, some hundreds of millions of guilders of bank loans were raised in the Netherlands.

Appendix E: Figures by country and by sector, 1973-1983

Geographical breakdown by sector of Netherlands direct investment abroad at end-1973
(millions of guilders)

Country or group of countries/sector	Agri-culture and fishing	Production industries					Con-struc-tion	Services					Grand total
		mining and quarrying, oil and chemicals	metals and electrical engineering	food, drink and tobacco	other	total		trade	transport, storage and communication	banking and insurance	other	total	
France	5	1,001	767	525	107	2,400	6	259	51	28	66	404	2,815
Belgium and Luxembourg	7	670	1,036	355	241	2,302	80	341	112	204	86	743	3,132
Federal Republic of Germany	2	1,950	3,279	2,185	76	7,490	40	532	75	60	125	792	8,324
Italy	3	194	233	240	52	719	–	56	3	–	22	81	803
United Kingdom	–	4,766	1,192	117	32	6,107	281	156	71	93	88	408	6,796
Ireland	–	64	24	14	4	106	2	1	2	8	1	12	120
Denmark	–	192	50	69	13	324	–	19	–	–	2	21	345
EC	17	8,837	6,581	3,505	525	19,448	409	1,364	314	393	390	2,461	22,335
United States	–	4,387	726	788	–8	5,893	–	243	–3	36	31	307	6,200
Switzerland	–	184	52	245	90	571	13	253	39	71	78	441	1,025
Other developed countries	11	3,922	1,226	376	83	5,607	21	77	117	320	6	520	6,159
Developing countries													
Europe	–	543	411	232	34	1,220	–8	10	5	2	8	25	1,237
Africa	96	–285	46	218	20	–1	7	68	25	6	–	99	201
Asia	2	1,032	407	200	3	1,642	–	46	25	20	3	94	1,738
Latin America	1	2,294	1,185	299	57	3,835	53	304	790	93	202	1,389	5,278
(of which: Netherlands Antilles)	(–)	(1,033)	(310)	(213)	(37)	(1,593)	(51)	(166)	(510)	(86)	(169)	(931)	(2,575)
Total developing countries	99	3,584	2,049	949	114	6,696	52	428	845	121	213	1,607	8,454
Grand total	127	20,914	10,634	5,863	804	38,215	495	2,365	1,312	941	718	5,336	44,173

Geographical breakdown by sector of Netherlands direct investment abroad at end-1974
(millions of guilders)

Country or group of countries/sector	Agri-culture and fishing	Production industries					Con-struc-tion	Services					Grand total
		mining and quarrying, oil and chemicals	metals and elec-trical engineer-ing	food, drink and tobacco	other	total		trade	trans-port, storage and communi-cation	banking and insur-ance	other	total	
France	4	1,408	820	579	120	2,927	29	329	57	34	97	517	3,477
Belgium and Luxembourg	5	767	1,128	419	307	2,621	102	382	154	324	117	977	3,705
Federal Republic of Germany	2	2,207	3,395	1,787	89	7,478	22	661	94	87	133	975	8,477
Italy	3	75	225	235	63	598	–	56	5	4	35	100	701
United Kingdom	1	7,473	1,207	134	87	8,901	293	229	69	106	99	503	9,698
Ireland	–	82	30	11	4	127	2	1	13	12	1	27	156
Denmark	–	196	52	81	15	344	–	18	–	4	10	32	376
EC	15	12,208	6,857	3,246	685	22,996	448	1,676	392	571	492	3,131	26,590
United States	–	4,447	1,126	789	1	6,363	–	137	7	88	26	258	6,621
Switzerland	–	228	68	198	126	620	15	298	81	142	91	612	1,247
Other developed countries	10	4,112	1,288	377	74	5,851	23	63	84	130	5	282	6,166
Developing countries													
Europe	–	617	454	236	42	1,349	6	13	4	5	14	36	1,391
Africa	87	-170	43	223	21	117	6	76	28	10	1	115	325
Asia	2	748	531	218	10	1,507	5	60	27	23	6	116	1,630
Latin America	3	1,970	1,263	589	72	3,894	74	297	976	124	284	1,681	5,652
(of which: Netherlands Antilles)	(–)	(1,040)	(325)	(486)	(37)	(1,888)	(70)	(148)	(699)	(110)	(445)	(1,402)	(3,360)
Total developing countries	92	3,165	2,291	1,266	145	6,867	91	446	1,035	162	305	1,948	8,998
Grand total	117	24,160	11,630	5,876	1,031	42,697	577	2,620	1,599	1,093	919	6,231	49,622

Geographical breakdown by sector of Netherlands direct investment abroad at end-1975
(millions of guilders)

Country or group of countries/sector	Agri-culture and fishing	Production industries					Con-struction	Services					Grand total
		mining and quarrying, oil and chemicals	metals and electrical engineering	food, drink and tobacco	other	total		trade	transport, storage and communication	banking and insurance	other	total	
France	12	1,221	960	600	121	2,902	25	337	45	48	201	631	3,570
Belgium and Luxembourg	7	920	1,230	502	366	3,018	150	338	179	346	101	964	4,139
Federal Republic of Germany	2	1,910	4,023	1,587	75	7,595	50	811	108	112	129	1,160	8,807
Italy	4	97	214	246	50	607	–	58	5	2	44	109	720
United Kingdom	1	7,714	1,312	137	77	9,240	319	190	87	164	98	539	10,099
Ireland	–	21	45	15	13	94	6	1	5	13	1	20	120
Denmark	2	359	62	87	12	520	–	19	1	−1	10	29	551
EC	28	12,242	7,846	3,174	714	23,976	550	1,754	430	684	584	3,452	28,006
United States	–	4,297	1,505	873	4	6,679	–	177	31	179	60	447	7,126
Switzerland	2	271	192	248	134	845	20	377	92	143	89	701	1,568
Other developed countries	3	4,540	1,367	382	56	6,345	17	81	57	123	77	338	6,703
Developing countries													
Europe	–	632	531	264	37	1,464	29	24	3	5	30	62	1,555
Africa	94	105	65	175	32	377	2	83	35	8	2	128	601
Asia	5	1,059	468	239	10	1,776	1	67	34	34	6	141	1,923
Latin America	5	1,772	1,570	708	65	4,115	218	327	976	146	292	1,741	6,079
(of which: Netherlands Antilles)	(1)	(1,199)	(370)	(590)	(37)	(2,196)	(190)	(151)	(872)	(130)	(264)	(1,417)	(3,804)
Total developing countries	104	3,568	2,634	1,386	144	7,732	250	501	1,048	193	330	2,072	10,158
Grand total	137	24,918	13,544	6,063	1,052	45,577	837	2,890	1,658	1,322	1,140	7,010	53,561

Geographical breakdown by sector of Netherlands direct investment abroad at end-1976
(millions of guilders)

Country or group of countries/sector	Agri-culture and fishing	Production industries					Con-struc-tion	Services					Grand total
		mining and quarrying, oil and chemicals	metals and electrical engineering	food, drink and tobacco	other	total		trade	transport, storage and communication	banking and insurance	other	total	
France	10	1,219	817	615	108	2,759	26	266	41	86	147	540	3,335
Belgium and Luxembourg	15	969	1,410	553	440	3,372	144	454	195	334	177	1,160	4,691
Federal Republic of Germany	4	1,364	3,861	1,481	63	6,769	21	662	115	140	164	1,081	7,875
Italy	–	88	241	255	22	606	7	36	6	–	66	108	721
United Kingdom	1	6,007	977	229	90	7,303	254	229	66	151	60	506	8,064
Ireland	–	41	40	10	11	102	5	1	6	11	–	18	125
Denmark	6	200	69	57	12	338	–	17	2	–	10	29	373
EC	36	9,888	7,415	3,200	746	21,249	457	1,665	431	722	624	3,442	25,184
United States	–	4,805	1,489	888	33	7,215	5	240	121	242	102	705	7,925
Switzerland	1	208	258	305	106	877	23	466	90	154	174	884	1,785
Other developed countries	2	3,769	1,406	426	62	5,663	19	100	40	118	73	331	6,015
Developing countries													
Europe	-1	500	513	255	43	1,311	26	21	4	2	33	60	1,396
Africa	94	130	95	199	20	444	75	85	11	6	2	104	717
Asia	5	1,113	471	255	8	1,847	10	65	39	49	4	157	2,019
Latin America	5	1,753	1,622	748	200	4,323	347	388	904	156	353	1,801	6,476
(of which: Netherlands Antilles)	(–)	(1,042)	(337)	(607)	(155)	(2,141)	(328)	(225)	(845)	(141)	(299)	(1,510)	(3,979)
Total developing countries	103	3,496	2,701	1,457	271	7,925	458	559	958	213	392	2,122	10,608
Grand total	142	22,166	13,269	6,276	1,218	42,929	962	3,030	1,640	1,449	1,365	7,484	51,517

Geographical breakdown by sector of Netherlands direct investment abroad at end-1977
(millions of guilders)

Country or group of countries/sector	Agri-cul-ture and fishing	Production industries					Con-struc-tion	Services					Grand total
		mining and quarrying, oil and chemicals	metals and elec-trical engineer-ing	food, drink and tobacco	other	total		trade	trans-port, storage and communi-cation	banking and insur-ance	other	total	
France	10	1,854	958	614	148	3,574	18	353	50	99	261	763	4,365
Belgium and Luxembourg	16	524	1,426	673	389	3,012	160	409	225	382	242	1,258	4,446
Federal Republic of Germany	7	1,849	4,110	1,512	88	7,559	41	648	116	162	379	1,305	8,912
Italy	1	115	315	259	24	713	9	58	7	–	65	130	853
United Kingdom	2	4,851	1,170	239	155	6,415	214	210	72	203	155	640	7,271
Ireland	–	–16	47	14	10	55	5	1	1	17	1	20	80
Denmark	2	409	64	49	13	535	–	–2	3	–	10	11	548
EC	38	9,586	8,090	3,360	827	21,863	447	1,677	474	863	1,113	4,127	26,475
United States	1	6,984	1,527	1,021	48	9,580	7	290	145	414	78	927	10,515
Switzerland	1	986	341	616	109	2,052	21	559	122	223	243	1,147	3,221
Other developed countries	2	4,126	1,394	408	91	6,019	17	51	31	119	84	285	6,323
Developing countries													
Europe	–	468	522	258	38	1,286	26	24	4	2	30	60	1,372
Africa	94	114	162	194	14	484	125	83	15	6	2	106	809
Asia	5	1,163	489	273	7	1,932	21	64	57	38	4	163	2,121
Latin America	8	1,658	1,550	914	241	4,363	548	535	866	208	441	2,050	6,969
(of which: Netherlands Antilles)	(3)	(237)	(202)	(782)	(211)	(1,432)	(530)	(382)	(817)	(177)	(391)	(1,767)	(3,732)
Total developing countries	107	3,403	2,723	1,639	300	8,065	720	706	942	254	477	2,379	11,271
Grand total	149	25,085	14,075	7,044	1,375	47,579	1,212	3,283	1,714	1,873	1,995	8,865	57,805

Geographical breakdown by sector of Netherlands direct investment abroad at end-1978
(millions of guilders)

Country or group of countries/sector	Agriculture and fishing	Production industries					Construction	Services					Grand total
		mining and quarrying, oil and chemicals	metals and electrical engineering	food, drink and tobacco	other	total		trade	transport, storage and communication	banking and insurance	other	total	
France	12	1,538	1,056	644	116	3,354	27	315	34	106	327	782	4,175
Belgium and Luxembourg	20	633	1,417	628	339	3,017	183	400	251	463	294	1,408	4,628
Federal Republic of Germany	14	1,558	4,665	1,640	92	7,955	67	655	104	167	476	1,402	9,438
Italy	2	161	338	285	26	810	9	56	5	1	48	110	931
United Kingdom	54	6,456	1,127	328	141	8,052	166	200	53	203	214	670	8,942
Ireland	–	56	53	22	7	138	13	1	2	17	24	44	195
Denmark	2	240	64	55	13	372	–	9	2	–	9	20	394
EC	104	10,642	8,720	3,602	734	23,698	465	1,636	451	957	1,392	4,436	28,703
United States	96	6,516	1,429	1,725	50	9,720	27	361	95	372	110	938	10,781
Switzerland	2	229	386	847	120	1,582	10	909	117	251	498	1,775	3,369
Other developed countries	5	3,960	1,300	317	80	5,657	17	72	24	110	56	262	5,941
Developing countries													
Europe	–	464	561	245	45	1,315	13	28	5	2	28	63	1,391
Africa	95	243	152	179	24	598	80	71	16	6	1	94	867
Asia	3	1,101	529	254	4	1,888	–4	82	59	144	5	290	2,177
Latin America	7	1,649	1,583	977	268	4,477	516	879	729	314	421	2,343	7,343
(of which: Netherlands Antilles)	(3)	(719)	(202)	(727)	(237)	(1,885)	(496)	(701)	(700)	(282)	(347)	(2,030)	(4,414)
Total developing countries	105	3,457	2,825	1,655	341	8,278	605	1,060	809	466	455	2,790	11,778
Grand total	312	24,804	14,660	8,146	1,325	48,935	1,124	4,038	1,496	2,156	2,511	10,201	60,572

Geographical breakdown by sector of Netherlands direct investment abroad at end-1979
(millions of guilders)

Country or group of countries/sector	Agriculture and fishing	Production industries					Construction	Services					Grand total
		mining and quarrying, oil and chemicals	metals and electrical engineering	food, drink and tobacco	other	total		trade	transport, storage and communication	banking and insurance	other	total	
France	17	2,223	1,163	617	132	4,135	54	278	67	159	403	907	5,113
Belgium and Luxembourg	23	1,200	1,736	643	456	4,035	218	483	185	510	290	1,468	5,744
Federal Republic of Germany	13	2,588	4,208	1,462	126	8,384	45	684	104	207	429	1,424	9,866
Italy	2	149	359	285	37	830	8	73	5	9	57	144	984
United Kingdom	125	7,927	1,283	409	163	9,782	188	248	106	192	246	792	10,887
Ireland	–	147	87	22	17	273	12	23	2	16	18	59	344
Denmark	3	367	69	56	7	499	–1	16	2	–	12	30	531
EC	183	14,601	8,905	3,494	938	27,938	524	1,805	471	1,093	1,455	4,824	33,469
United States	122	7,739	1,599	2,016	117	11,471	41	597	149	582	564	1,892	13,526
Switzerland	2	374	399	980	118	1,871	80	1,254	129	277	407	2,067	4,020
Other developed countries	4	5,304	1,302	326	89	7,021	21	104	14	121	53	292	7,338
Developing countries													
Europe	–	555	801	319	54	1,729	4	31	5	16	38	90	1,823
Africa	94	326	170	104	28	628	54	75	16	6	–	97	873
Asia	4	1,511	615	291	5	2,422	–14	99	82	173	4	358	2,770
Latin America	7	2,135	1,756	999	382	5,272	633	866	629	340	408	2,243	8,155
(of which: Netherlands Antilles)	(3)	(1,141)	(962)	(695)	(336)	(3,134)	(591)	(682)	(587)	(303)	(356)	(1,928)	(5,656)
Total developing countries	105	4,527	3,342	1,713	469	10,051	677	1,071	732	535	450	2,788	13,621
Grand total	416	32,545	15,547	8,529	1,731	58,352	1,343	4,831	1,495	2,608	2,929	11,863	71,974

Geographical breakdown by sector of Netherlands direct investment abroad at end-1980
(millions of guilders)

Country or group of countries/sector	Agriculture and fishing	Production industries					Construction	Services					Grand total
		mining and quarrying, oil and chemicals	metals and electrical engineering	food, drink and tobacco	other	total		trade	transport, storage and communication	banking and insurance	other	total	
France	14	3,014	1,244	579	138	4,975	45	298	76	192	569	1,135	6,169
Belgium and Luxembourg	96	1,390	1,741	553	603	4,287	255	578	199	517	413	1,707	6,345
Federal Republic of Germany	9	2,741	4,414	764	150	8,069	42	811	104	222	549	1,686	9,806
Italy	3	165	391	268	45	869	8	99	6	9	328	442	1,322
United Kingdom	104	14,350	1,696	372	152	16,570	145	235	81	243	624	1,183	18,002
Ireland	–	308	90	36	7	441	12	18	2	16	19	55	508
Denmark	2	495	206	79	7	787	−4	18	2	–	8	28	813
EC	228	22,463	9,782	2,651	1,102	35,998	503	2,057	470	1,199	2,510	6,236	42,965
United States	69	10,575	1,915	1,493	73	14,056	16	1,059	169	879	616	2,723	16,864
Switzerland	17	374	286	1,002	130	1,792	100	1,341	137	411	418	2,307	4,216
Other developed countries	4	6,258	1,698	297	123	8,376	33	191	12	234	110	547	8,960
Developing countries													
Europe	8	576	714	232	59	1,581	−3	26	5	31	53	115	1,701
Africa	89	354	162	86	29	631	32	71	12	6	2	91	843
Asia	11	2,503	752	370	8	3,633	−43	81	107	178	24	390	3,991
Latin America	13	2,691	2,085	972	388	6,136	551	1,723	579	376	767	3,445	10,145
(of which: Netherlands Antilles)	(3)	(1,086)	(862)	(633)	(357)	(2,938)	(499)	(1,504)	(546)	(340)	(569)	(2,959)	(6,399)
Total developing countries	121	6,124	3,713	1,660	484	11,981	537	1,901	703	591	846	4,041	16,680
Grand total	439	45,794	17,394	7,103	1,912	72,203	1,189	6,549	1,491	3,314	4,500	15,854	89,685

Geographical breakdown by sector of Netherlands direct investment abroad at end-1981
(millions of guilders)

Country or group of countries/sector	Agriculture and fishing	Production industries					Construction	Services					Grand total
		mining and quarrying, oil and chemicals	metals and electrical engineering	food, drink and tobacco	other	total		trade	transport, storage and communication	banking and insurance	other	total	
France	27	2,184	1,312	619	127	4,242	42	333	73	171	511	1,088	5,399
Belgium and Luxembourg	96	1,495	1,752	615	503	4,365	301	594	231	720	469	2,014	6,776
Federal Republic of Germany	19	3,025	3,805	1,004	146	7,980	26	722	79	250	631	1,682	9,707
Italy	5	184	478	319	27	1,008	8	125	1	9	669	804	1,825
United Kingdom	72	14,657	1,470	237	82	16,446	70	339	71	231	474	1,115	17,703
Ireland	1	688	94	59	3	844	12	17	3	22	22	64	921
Denmark	2	555	76	494	7	1,132	-5	29	2	21	6	58	1,187
EC	222	22,788	8,987	3,347	895	36,017	454	2,159	460	1,424	2,782	6,825	43,518
United States	68	12,691	2,546	1,733	158	17,128	27	1,208	259	1,450	1,401	4,318	21,541
Switzerland	6	457	570	681	158	1,866	104	1,310	154	500	508	2,472	4,448
Other developed countries	2	7,735	2,022	403	150	10,310	50	272	9	482	188	951	11,313
Developing countries													
Europe	32	454	655	287	69	1,465	4	33	11	27	39	110	1,611
Africa	93	546	112	83	12	753	66	83	15	6	36	140	1,052
Asia	6	2,518	947	601	10	4,076	-9	85	128	158	53	424	4,497
Latin America	208	2,699	2,290	1,271	419	6,679	836	1,925	514	371	995	3,805	11,528
(of which: Netherlands Antilles)	(18)	(1,074)	(895)	(790)	(392)	(3,151)	(707)	(1,683)	(476)	(329)	(913)	(3,401)	(7,277)
Total developing countries	339	6,217	4,004	2,242	510	12,973	897	2,126	668	562	1,123	4,479	18,688
Grand total	637	49,888	18,129	8,406	1,871	78,294	1,532	7,075	1,550	4,418	6,002	19,045	99,508

Geographical breakdown by sector of Netherlands direct investment abroad at end-1982
(millions of guilders)

Country or group of countries/sector	Agri-cul-ture and fishing	Production industries					Con-struc-tion	Services					Grand total
		mining and quarrying, oil and chemicals	metals and elec-trical engineer-ing	food, drink and tobacco	other	total		trade	trans-port, storage and communi-cation	banking and insur-ance	other	total	
France	40	2,033	1,231	558	104	3,926	11	305	83	123	405	916	4,893
Belgium and Luxembourg	81	1,185	1,466	638	358	3,647	396	908	188	887	992	2,975	7,099
Federal Republic of Germany	298	2,953	1,714	1,182	218	6,067	45	670	138	276	600	1,684	8,094
Italy	5	147	500	371	16	1,034	7	127	5	30	115	277	1,323
United Kingdom	70	16,074	1,293	192	64	17,623	192	473	98	267	484	1,322	19,207
Ireland	–	849	86	88	-8	1,015	14	19	2	21	23	65	1,094
Denmark	3	783	75	45	10	913	-4	40	1	31	4	76	988
EC	497	24,024	6,365	3,074	762	34,225	661	2,542	515	1,635	2,623	7,315	42,698
United States	205	14,421	2,809	2,053	141	19,424	11	1,375	259	2,405	2,148	6,187	25,827
Switzerland	6	437	683	1,162	198	2,480	89	1,054	101	529	743	2,427	5,002
Other developed countries	3	7,702	1,853	364	137	10,056	53	286	11	461	107	865	10,977
Developing countries													
Europe	3	434	563	338	59	1,394	-9	59	7	35	96	197	1,585
Africa	–	890	105	94	47	1,136	104	93	14	6	32	145	1,385
Asia	2	3,166	780	608	9	4,563	-101	161	151	325	55	692	5,156
Latin America	6	2,422	2,111	1,258	452	6,243	778	2,433	421	427	1,353	4,634	11,661
(of which: Netherlands Antilles)	(5)	(884)	(600)	(701)	(432)	(2,617)	(629)	(1,961)	(383)	(403)	(1,286)	(4,033)	(7,284)
Total developing countries	11	6,912	3,559	2,298	567	13,336	772	2,746	593	793	1,536	5,668	19,787
Grand total	722	53,496	15,269	8,951	1,805	79,521	1,586	8,003	1,479	5,823	7,157	22,462	104,291

Geographical breakdown by sector of Netherlands direct investment abroad at end-1983
(millions of guilders)

Country or group of countries/sector	Agri-cul-ture and fishing	Production industries					Con-struc-tion	Services					Grand total
		mining and quarrying, oil and chemicals	metals and elec-trical engineer-ing	food, drink and tobacco	other	total		trade	trans-port, storage and communi-cation	banking and insur-ance	other	total	
France	48	1,512	1,140	704	67	3,423	21	765	81	75	360	1,281	4,773
Belgium and Luxembourg	40	1,395	1,752	673	362	4,182	325	985	206	948	775	2,914	7,461
Federal Republic of Germany	27	3,058	1,966	1,193	187	6,404	60	629	116	524	605	1,874	8,365
Italy	7	198	647	472	1	1,318	7	140	2	30	131	303	1,635
United Kingdom	192	17,193	1,501	160	–	18,854	153	480	68	537	785	1,870	21,069
Ireland	3	1,451	65	72	-6	1,582	10	16	5	17	24	62	1,657
Denmark	3	1,079	77	60	1	1,217	-13	42	2	47	5	96	1,303
EC	320	25,886	7,148	3,334	612	36,980	563	3,057	480	2,178	2,685	8,400	46,263
United States	330	19,084	3,708	2,585	121	25,498	88	1,494	295	2,992	2,701	7,482	33,398
Switzerland	6	699	891	1,128	235	2,953	78	996	111	504	792	2,403	5,440
Other developed countries	72	9,683	2,213	496	66	12,458	77	448	1	698	130	1,277	13,884
Developing countries													
Europe	4	507	554	338	32	1,431	-9	45	1	37	118	201	1,627
Africa	–	1,151	80	114	35	1,380	159	93	12	6	30	141	1,680
Asia	2	3,950	1,053	599	8	5,610	-273	182	181	403	39	805	6,144
Latin America	3	2,896	1,620	688	459	5,663	756	2,763	379	548	1,338	5,028	11,450
(of which: Netherlands Antilles)	(3)	(1,082)	(324)	(172)	(460)	(2,038)	(604)	(2,264)	(342)	(477)	(1,268)	(4,351)	(6,996)
Total developing countries	9	8,504	3,307	1,739	534	14,084	633	3,083	573	994	1,525	6,175	20,901
Grand total	737	63,856	17,267	9,282	1,568	91,973	1,439	9,078	1,460	7,366	7,833	25,737	119,886

Geographical breakdown by sector of foreign direct investment in the Netherlands at end-1973
(millions of guilders)

Country or group of countries/sector	Agri-culture and fishing	Production industries					Con-struc-tion	Services					Grand total
		mining and quarrying, oil and chemicals	metals and elèc-trical engineer-ing	food, drink and tobacco	other	total		trade	trans-port, storage and communi-cation	banking and insur-ance	other	total	
France	–	437	76	8	135	656	6	98	8	141	25	272	934
Belgium and Luxembourg	–	293	330	121	181	925	114	351	57	45	22	475	1,514
Federal Republic of Germany	–	289	1,781	6	62	2,138	3	284	105	53	31	473	2,614
Italy	–	33	–4	–	–	29	–	29	1	12	2	44	73
United Kingdom	1	1,354	162	259	424	2,199	16	484	88	502	382	1,456	3,672
Ireland	–	–	1	–	3	4	–	–	–	–	18	18	22
Denmark	–	2	–	–	8	10	–	1	–	–	–	1	11
EC	1	2,408	2,346	394	813	5,961	139	1,247	259	753	480	2,739	8,840
United States	5	4,609	954	295	332	6,190	9	736	6	230	513	1,485	7,689
Switzerland	1	662	336	284	262	1,544	7	307	40	24	116	487	2,039
Japan	–	–	12	–	5	17	–	20	2	119	1	142	159
Other developed countries	2	89	163	35	133	420	7	277	13	–1	13	302	731
Developing countries													
Europe	–	–	–	–	–	–	–	7	1	2	–	10	10
Africa	–	392	–	–	–	392	–	2	2	–	–	4	396
Asia	–	–	4	1	–	5	–	3	–	38	5	46	51
Latin America	2	156	126	133	67	482	1	177	32	2	48	259	744
(of which: Netherlands Antilles)	(2)	(153)	(102)	(112)	(44)	(411)	(–1)	(167)	(–17)	(1)	(41)	(192)	(604)
Total developing countries	2	548	130	134	67	879	1	189	35	42	53	319	1,201
Grand total	11	8,316	3,941	1,142	1,612	15,011	163	2,776	355	1,167	1,176	5,474	20,659

Geographical breakdown by sector of foreign direct investment in the Netherlands at end-1974
(millions of guilders)

Country or group of countries/sector	Agri-culture and fishing	Production industries					Con-struc-tion	Services					Grand total
		mining and quarrying, oil and chemicals	metals and elec-trical engineer-ing	food, drink and tobacco	other	total		trade	trans-port, storage and communi-cation	banking and insur-ance	other	total	
France	–	542	87	9	135	773	9	109	10	144	14	277	1,059
Belgium and Luxembourg	–	259	461	149	183	1,052	139	365	58	56	36	515	1,706
Federal Republic of Germany	–	368	2,058	6	63	2,495	4	289	90	69	63	511	3,010
Italy	–	33	4	–	–	29	–	27	1	4	2	34	63
United Kingdom	1	2,040	177	232	467	2,916	16	505	92	500	457	1,553	4,487
Ireland	–	–	1	–	3	4	–	–	1	–	7	8	12
Denmark	–	2	–	–3	9	8	–	1	–	–	2	3	11
EC	1	3,244	2,780	393	860	7,277	168	1,296	252	773	581	2,902	10,348
United States	13	4,570	1,055	317	389	6,331	16	754	18	296	584	1,652	8,012
Switzerland	1	859	301	259	310	1,729	8	378	48	30	114	570	2,308
Japan	–	–	11	–	6	17	–	50	2	168	6	226	243
Other developed countries	1	102	173	36	157	468	8	309	79	17	7	412	889
Developing countries													
Europe	–	–	–	–	–1	–1	–	6	1	3	–	10	9
Africa	–	392	–	–	–	392	–	8	2	–	1	11	403
Asia	–	–	3	4	–	7	–	3	–	43	10	56	63
Latin America	2	690	154	134	72	1,050	6	202	72	13	67	354	1,412
(of which: Netherlands Antilles)	(2)	(153)	(134)	(112)	(54)	(453)	(5)	(202)	(7)	(2)	(59)	(270)	(730)
Total developing countries	2	1,082	157	138	71	1,448	6	219	75	59	78	431	1,887
Grand total	18	9,857	4,477	1,143	1,793	17,270	206	3,006	474	1,343	1,370	6,193	23,687

Geographical breakdown by sector of foreign direct investment in the Netherlands at end-1975
(millions of guilders)

Country or group of countries/sector	Agri-cul-ture and fishing	Production industries					Con-struc-tion	Services					Grand total
		mining and quarrying, oil and chemicals	metals and elec-trical engineer-ing	food, drink and tobacco	other	total		trade	trans-port, storage and communi-cation	banking and insur-ance	other	total	
France	5	532	28	–	146	706	8	82	10	189	202	483	1,202
Belgium and Luxembourg	–	300	373	144	218	1,035	141	289	55	23	41	408	1,584
Federal Republic of Germany	–	393	2,040	11	81	2,525	11	316	86	84	29	515	3,051
Italy	-4	24	-4	–	-1	19	–	5	1	14	9	29	44
United Kingdom	–	2,301	171	291	480	3,243	19	500	109	618	483	1,710	4,972
Ireland	–	–	–	–	24	24	–	–	1	–	–	1	25
Denmark	–	2	–	-5	17	14	–	-1	–	–	2	1	15
EC	1	3,552	2,608	441	965	7,566	179	1,191	262	928	766	3,147	10,893
United States	15	5,336	1,342	437	364	7,479	21	643	3	400	553	1,599	9,114
Switzerland	1	929	344	251	334	1,858	3	467	58	31	93	649	2,511
Japan	–	–	10	–	6	16	–	78	2	182	7	269	285
Other developed countries	14	83	349	16	152	600	9	323	65	24	32	444	1,067
Developing countries													
Europe	–	–	–	12	–	12	–	8	2	4	–	14	26
Africa	–	421	–	–	–	421	–	12	2	–	–	14	435
Asia	–	–	3	6	1	10	–	8	–	46	3	57	67
Latin America	2	704	166	208	76	1,154	19	394	176	22	217	809	1,984
(of which: Netherlands Antilles)	(2)	(139)	(146)	(201)	(59)	(545)	(17)	(350)	(112)	(6)	(214)	(682)	(1,246)
Total developing countries	2	1,125	169	226	77	1,597	19	422	180	72	220	894	2,512
Grand total	33	11,025	4,822	1,371	1,898	19,116	231	3,124	570	1,637	1,671	7,002	26,382

Geographical breakdown by sector of foreign direct investment in the Netherlands at end-1976
(millions of guilders)

Country or group of countries/sector	Agri-culture and fishing	Production industries					Con-struc-tion	Services					Grand total
		mining and quarrying, oil and chemicals	metals and elec-trical engineer-ing	food, drink and tobacco	other	total		trade	trans-port, storage and communi-cation	banking and insur-ance	other	total	
France	6	655	35	-3	101	788	2	89	9	203	134	435	1,231
Belgium and Luxembourg	–	192	402	157	217	968	83	249	53	23	67	392	1,443
Federal Republic of Germany	–	230	2,017	10	73	2,330	9	354	90	95	32	571	2,910
Italy	-2	37	–	–	–	37	–	8	1	15	106	130	165
United Kingdom	1	1,572	147	300	409	2,428	22	598	118	715	520	1,951	4,402
Ireland	–	5	–	–	22	27	–	–	–	–	–	–	27
Denmark	–	2	-1	-7	18	12	–	–	–	–	3	3	15
EC	5	2,693	2,600	457	840	6,590	116	1,298	271	1,051	862	3,482	10,193
United States	–	6,620	1,382	468	338	8,808	23	768	42	396	661	1,867	10,698
Switzerland	3	1,033	406	271	329	2,039	11	817	62	22	129	1,030	3,083
Japan	–	–	11	–	4	15	–	79	2	275	16	372	387
Other developed countries	16	124	463	20	160	767	11	411	47	27	36	521	1,315
Developing countries													
Europe	1	–	–	26	–	26	–	7	3	5	–	15	42
Africa	–	421	–	–	–	421	–	3	2	–	7	12	433
Asia	–	–	2	6	1	9	–	18	–	47	1	66	75
Latin America	2	445	161	202	130	938	71	454	134	103	498	1,189	2,200
(of which: Netherlands Antilles)	(2)	(118)	(133)	(179)	(116)	(546)	(70)	(412)	(73)	(91)	(483)	(1,059)	(1,677)
Total developing countries	3	866	163	234	131	1,394	71	482	139	155	506	1,282	2,750
Grand total	27	11,336	5,025	1,450	1,802	19,613	232	3,855	563	1,926	2,210	8,554	28,426

Geographical breakdown by sector of foreign direct investment in the Netherlands at end-1977
(millions of guilders)

Country or group of countries/sector	Agri-culture and fishing	Production industries					Con-struc-tion	Services					Grand total
		mining and quarrying, oil and chemicals	metals and electrical engineering	food, drink and tobacco	other	total		trade	transport, storage and communication	banking and insurance	other	total	
France	6	509	13	–	80	602	6	103	10	264	119	496	1,110
Belgium and Luxembourg	–	103	375	121	252	851	92	277	15	5	98	395	1,338
Federal Republic of Germany	2	343	1,798	11	102	2,254	3	467	106	107	35	715	2,974
Italy	-3	39	-1	–	–	38	–	27	3	20	8	58	93
United Kingdom	1	1,774	147	337	422	2,680	10	571	92	875	614	2,152	4,843
Ireland	–	5	–	–	18	23	–	–	2	–	–	2	25
Denmark	–	1	–	-13	26	14	–	3	–	5	7	15	29
EC	6	2,774	2,332	456	900	6,462	111	1,448	228	1,276	881	3,833	10,412
United States	–	6,335	1,458	582	1,007	9,382	21	849	42	357	705	1,953	11,356
Switzerland	3	1,106	606	266	306	2,284	2	834	73	12	209	1,128	3,417
Japan	–	9	10	–	5	24	–	111	2	315	16	444	468
Other developed countries	34	132	417	24	172	745	15	321	25	29	69	444	1,238
Developing countries													
Europe	1	–	–	–	–	–	–	6	3	4	–	13	14
Africa	–	421	–	–	–	421	–	1	4	–	4	9	430
Asia	–	–	-1	7	–	6	–	20	1	84	3	108	114
Latin America	2	679	180	276	145	1,280	43	571	145	108	581	1,405	2,730
(of which: Netherlands Antilles)	(2)	(148)	(152)	(224)	(123)	(647)	(38)	(512)	(80)	(96)	(563)	(1,251)	(1,938)
Total developing countries	3	1,100	179	283	145	1,707	43	598	153	196	588	1,535	3,288
Grand total	46	11,456	5,002	1,611	2,535	20,604	192	4,161	523	2,185	2,468	9,337	30,179

Geographical breakdown by sector of foreign direct investment in the Netherlands at end-1978
(millions of guilders)

Country or group of countries/sector	Agri-culture and fishing	Production industries					Con-struc-tion	Services					Grand total
		mining and quarrying, oil and chemicals	metals and elec-trical engineer-ing	food, drink and tobacco	other	total		trade	trans-port, storage and communi-cation	banking and insur-ance	other	total	
France	3	509	212	1	80	802	7	108	10	296	124	538	1,350
Belgium and Luxembourg	5	308	520	98	278	1,204	80	349	20	1	175	545	1,834
Federal Republic of Germany	3	291	1,561	9	96	1,957	2	494	213	88	67	862	2,824
Italy	-2	-	-1	2	-	1	-	25	2	15	24	66	65
United Kingdom	1	976	194	359	451	1,980	17	481	63	988	744	2,276	4,274
Ireland	-	5	-	-	5	10	-	-	1	-	2	3	13
Denmark	-	2	1	1	35	39	-	3	1	-	10	14	53
EC	10	2,091	2,487	470	945	5,993	106	1,460	310	1,388	1,146	4,304	10,413
United States	-	6,092	2,355	965	416	9,828	13	1,075	22	272	299	1,668	11,509
Switzerland	-	1,069	549	549	356	2,523	2	1,352	52	12	150	1,566	4,091
Japan	-	8	9	-	5	22	-	117	2	344	13	476	498
Other developed countries	52	97	552	22	172	843	3	350	66	28	65	509	1,407
Developing countries													
Europe	1	-	1	-	-	1	-	17	5	-1	-	21	23
Africa	-	265	-	-	-	265	-	-1	1	-	3	3	268
Asia	-	-	-1	8	-	7	-	17	-	93	3	113	120
Latin America	70	483	178	280	100	1,041	110	845	182	36	952	2,015	3,236
(of which: Netherlands Antilles)	(63)	(159)	(117)	(213)	(77)	(566)	(105)	(802)	(160)	(25)	(841)	(1,828)	(2,562)
Total developing countries	71	748	178	288	100	1,314	110	878	188	128	958	2,152	3,647
Grand total	133	10,105	6,130	2,294	1,994	20,523	234	5,232	640	2,172	2,631	10,675	31,565

Geographical breakdown by sector of foreign direct investment in the Netherlands at end-1979
(millions of guilders)

Country or group of countries/sector	Agri-culture and fishing	Production industries: mining and quarrying, oil and chemicals	Production industries: metals and electrical engineering	Production industries: food, drink and tobacco	Production industries: other	Production industries: total	Con-struc-tion	Services: trade	Services: transport, storage and communication	Services: banking and insurance	Services: other	Services: total	Grand total
France	-1	323	244	7	94	668	5	120	11	325	192	648	1,320
Belgium and Luxembourg	4	354	964	107	332	1,757	13	366	28	7	246	647	2,421
Federal Republic of Germany	3	272	1,335	18	142	1,767	2	502	187	95	91	875	2,647
Italy	-3	22	4	2	1	29	-	28	2	15	32	77	103
United Kingdom	-	1,375	292	461	478	2,606	19	575	56	1,124	1,093	2,848	5,473
Ireland	-	6	-	-	6	12	-	-	-	-	3	3	15
Denmark	1	4	8	1	42	55	-	2	1	-	6	9	65
EC	4	2,356	2,847	596	1,095	6,894	39	1,593	285	1,566	1,663	5,107	12,044
United States	-	6,832	2,521	1,010	432	10,795	16	815	39	358	425	1,637	12,448
Switzerland	5	1,160	619	561	336	2,676	2	1,421	71	11	224	1,727	4,410
Japan	-	5	14	-	5	24	-	113	2	419	14	548	572
Other developed countries	53	141	593	24	154	912	3	807	10	13	75	905	1,873
Developing countries													
Europe	1	-	3	-	-	3	-	21	6	25	-	52	56
Africa	-	349	2	-	-	351	-	3	2	-	5	10	361
Asia	-	1	-	10	1	12	-	17	1	96	4	118	130
Latin America	93	384	168	341	135	1,028	163	1,354	173	45	1,397	2,969	4,253
(of which: Netherlands Antilles)	(69)	(161)	(83)	(220)	(89)	(553)	(121)	(1,219)	(130)	(25)	(992)	(2,366)	(3,109)
Total developing countries	94	734	173	351	136	1,394	163	1,395	182	166	1,406	3,149	4,800
Grand total	156	11,228	6,767	2,542	2,158	22,695	223	6,144	589	2,533	3,807	13,073	36,147

Geographical breakdown by sector of foreign direct investment in the Netherlands at end-1980
(millions of guilders)

Country or group of countries/sector	Agri-cul-ture and fishing	Production industries					Con-struc-tion	Services					Grand total
		mining and quarrying, oil and chemicals	metals and elec-trical engineer-ing	food, drink and tobacco	other	total		trade	trans-port, storage and communi-cation	banking and insur-ance	other	total	
France	1	384	269	7	101	761	6	126	12	347	201	686	1,454
Belgium and Luxembourg	13	351	991	104	344	1,790	7	383	35	11	219	648	2,458
Federal Republic of Germany	6	420	1,168	26	103	1,717	1	455	184	139	617	1,395	3,119
Italy	-4	10	11	2	5	28	–	15	3	19	13	50	74
United Kingdom	9	1,540	271	520	504	2,835	41	486	76	1,211	1,202	2,975	5,860
Ireland	–	1	–	–	–	1	–	–	1	–	1	2	3
Denmark	1	4	9	–	49	62	–	11	–	–	4	15	78
EC	26	2,710	2,719	659	1,106	7,194	55	1,476	311	1,727	2,257	5,771	13,046
United States	28	8,291	2,180	1,097	512	12,080	13	961	51	437	464	1,913	14,034
Switzerland	44	1,185	725	626	249	2,785	2	1,357	95	13	263	1,728	4,559
Japan	1	2	21	–	8	31	–	110	2	433	17	562	594
Other developed countries	51	149	725	43	64	981	1	784	36	14	120	954	1,987
Developing countries													
Europe	1	–	2	–	–	2	–	14	7	18	–	39	42
Africa	–	279	2	–	–	281	–	1	2	–	3	6	287
Asia	–	1	–	9	2	12	–	14	1	139	9	163	175
Latin America	151	301	236	362	132	1,031	240	2,610	248	55	1,758	4,671	6,093
(of which: Netherlands Antilles)	(137)	(158)	(155)	(273)	(107)	(693)	(235)	(2,085)	(229)	(31)	(1,660)	(4,005)	(5,070)
Total developing countries	152	581	240	371	134	1,326	240	2,639	258	212	1,770	4,879	6,597
Grand total	302	12,918	6,610	2,796	2,073	24,397	311	7,327	753	2,836	4,891	15,807	40,817

Geographical breakdown by sector of foreign direct investment in the Netherlands at end-1981
(millions of guilders)

Country or group of countries/sector	Agri-culture and fishing	Production industries					Con-struc-tion	Services					Grand total
		mining and quarrying, oil and chemicals	metals and elec-trical engineer-ing	food, drink and tobacco	other	total		trade	trans-port, storage and communi-cation	banking and insur-ance	other	total	
France	8	318	259	6	104	687	–	139	14	851	233	1,237	1,932
Belgium and Luxembourg	28	487	832	107	259	1,685	9	504	70	29	259	862	2,584
Federal Republic of Germany	19	455	963	35	131	1,584	2	491	236	149	737	1,613	3,218
Italy	–4	44	11	–	4	59	–	21	5	20	25	71	126
United Kingdom	247	2,149	315	563	244	3,271	41	943	84	1,339	1,037	3,403	6,962
Ireland	4	–	–	–	–2	–2	–	–	–	–	–	–	2
Denmark	–	4	8	1	43	56	–	75	–	–	3	78	134
EC	302	3,457	2,388	712	783	7,340	52	2,173	409	2,388	2,294	7,264	14,958
United States	61	9,573	2,108	1,223	424	13,328	15	933	50	491	580	2,054	15,458
Switzerland	159	1,237	711	631	439	3,018	2	1,165	34	18	296	1,513	4,692
Japan	9	8	34	–	29	71	–	125	2	523	22	672	752
Other developed countries	82	188	636	35	48	907	1	664	16	15	316	1,011	2,001
Developing countries													
Europe	1	–	3	–	–	3	–	4	8	19	9	40	44
Africa	–	339	2	–	–	341	–	5	–	–	–	5	346
Asia	15	1	1	19	3	24	–	14	1	134	11	160	199
Latin America	290	240	242	404	178	1,064	206	3,145	268	47	1,962	5,422	6,982
(of which: Netherlands Antilles)	(253)	(126)	(179)	(303)	(157)	(765)	(191)	(2,574)	(244)	(27)	(1,862)	(4,707)	(5,916)
Total developing countries	306	580	248	423	181	1,432	206	3,168	277	200	1,982	5,627	7,571
Grand total	919	15,043	6,125	3,024	1,904	26,096	276	8,228	788	3,635	5,490	18,141	45,432

Geographical breakdown by sector of foreign direct investment in the Netherlands at end-1982
(millions of guilders)

Country or group of countries/sector	Agriculture and fishing	Production industries					Construction	Services					Grand total
		mining and quarrying, oil and chemicals	metals and electrical engineering	food, drink and tobacco	other	total		trade	transport, storage and communication	banking and insurance	other	total	
France	5	360	387	10	106	863	–	276	19	861	291	1,447	2,315
Belgium and Luxembourg	46	331	281	99	243	954	19	542	66	11	350	969	1,988
Federal Republic of Germany	35	486	359	45	107	997	47	658	253	186	434	1,531	2,610
Italy	-6	76	3	1	4	84	–	20	5	24	35	84	162
United Kingdom	35	2,292	160	664	408	3,524	49	1,113	89	1,564	1,155	3,921	7,529
Ireland	2	–	–	–	-5	-5	–	–	–	7	154	161	158
Denmark	–	2	10	–	41	53	–	77	1	–	2	80	133
EC	117	3,547	1,200	819	904	6,470	115	2,686	433	2,653	2,421	8,193	14,895
United States	123	9,232	2,369	1,132	280	13,013	19	1,422	87	632	882	3,023	16,178
Switzerland	255	1,057	552	886	275	2,770	7	1,312	63	30	434	1,839	4,871
Japan	2	11	29	–	17	57	–	353	4	647	14	1,018	1,077
Other developed countries	91	168	658	41	82	949	4	592	37	17	324	970	2,014
Developing countries													
Europe	–	–	2	–	–	2	–	10	1	35	9	55	57
Africa	–	384	3	–	–	387	–	4	–	–	–	4	391
Asia	39	1	–	21	19	41	–	37	1	155	12	205	285
Latin America	219	263	388	421	237	1,309	253	3,299	264	58	2,006	5,627	7,408
(of which: Netherlands Antilles)	(170)	(168)	(286)	(305)	(214)	(973)	(223)	(2,723)	(240)	(36)	(1,900)	(4,899)	(6,265)
Total developing countries	258	648	393	442	256	1,739	253	3,350	266	248	2,027	5,891	8,141
Grand total	846	14,663	5,201	3,320	1,814	24,998	398	9,715	890	4,227	6,102	20,934	47,176

Geographical breakdown by sector of foreign direct investment in the Netherlands at end-1983
(millions of guilders)

Country or group of countries/sector	Agriculture and fishing	Production industries					Construction	Services					Grand total
		mining and quarrying, oil and chemicals	metals and electrical engineering	food, drink and tobacco	other	total		trade	transport, storage and communication	banking and insurance	other	total	
France	6	352	373	3	110	838	4	286	19	922	311	1,538	2,386
Belgium and Luxembourg	18	271	1,064	94	256	1,685	11	498	34	11	343	886	2,600
Federal Republic of Germany	21	725	383	41	89	1,238	44	708	64	145	655	1,572	2,875
Italy	-3	78	-1	1	4	82	-	1	11	35	36	83	162
United Kingdom	91	2,216	204	731	485	3,636	48	1,302	100	1,769	974	4,145	7,920
Ireland	1	-	1	-	3	4	-	1	2	13	198	214	219
Denmark	-	4	12	-1	43	58	-	96	1	-	2	99	157
EC	134	3,646	2,036	869	990	7,541	107	2,892	231	2,895	2,519	8,537	16,319
United States	81	10,395	2,438	1,251	426	14,510	17	1,781	70	815	746	3,412	18,020
Switzerland	152	1,453	784	1,000	359	3,596	11	1,257	75	25	554	1,911	5,670
Japan	-	14	31	-	146	191	-	381	4	698	17	1,100	1,291
Other developed countries	99	150	677	49	110	986	4	505	-7	21	443	962	2,051
Developing countries													
Europe	1	-	2	-	1	3	-	11	-	33	8	52	56
Africa	-	89	3	-	-	92	-	43	-	-	-	43	135
Asia	40	266	150	21	20	457	4	42	2	253	12	309	810
Latin America	272	471	353	435	244	1,503	288	2,898	180	61	2,311	5,450	7,513
(of which: Netherlands Antilles)	(228)	(204)	(260)	(243)	(224)	(931)	(261)	(2,522)	(169)	(38)	(2,138)	(4,867)	(6,287)
Total developing countries	313	826	508	456	265	2,055	292	2,994	182	347	2,331	5,854	8,514
Grand total	779	16,484	6,474	3,625	2,296	28,879	431	9,810	555	4,801	6,610	21,776	51,865

Bibliography

Acquino, A., 1978, Intra-industry trade and inter-industry specialization as concurrent sources of international trade in manufactures, *Weltwirtschaftliches Archiv*, pp. 275-296.

Andriessen, J.E., 1985, Multinationale ondernemingen, in: *Ondernemen in Nederland*, Kluwer, Deventer.

Bosch, K.D., 1948, *De Nederlandse beleggingen in de Verenigde Staten*, Elsevier, Amsterdam-Brussels.

Buck, R. 1985, *Nieuwe Japanse en Amerikaanse industriële vestigingen in West-Europa*, Nijmegen, July.

Bulcke, D. van den, 1985, Intragroepshandel van multinationale ondernemingen: empirische gegevens en handelspolitieke gevolgen, *Maandschrift Economie*, jaargang 49.

Business Week, 1985, August 20.

H.R.H. Prince Claus, 1985, Protectionisme Westerse wereld is kortzichtig en economisch dom, Speech at the Annual Meeting of the Netherlands Finance Company for Developing Countries at The Hague on May 2, *Nederlandse Staatscourant*, May 3.

Dekker, W., 1985, High-tech and the changing shape of world trade, *World Trade Conference*, Amsterdam, September 5.

Dunning, J.H., 1982, A note on intra-industry foreign direct investment, *Quarterly Review*, Banca Nazionale Del Lavoro, December.

Dunning, J.H., 1981, Explaining the international direct investment position of countries: towards a dynamic or developmental approach, *Weltwirtschaftliches Archiv*, Heft 1, pp. 30-64.

The Economist, 1983, Business Brief, May 21, pp. 98-99.

Ellsworth, R.R., 1985, Capital markets and competitive decline, *Harvard Business Review*, September-October.

FEM, 1985, Gevecht om de wereldmarkt, September 7.

FEM-trends, 1985, April 13.

Goldsbrough, D.J., 1985, Foreign private investment in developing countries, *IMF Occasional Paper*, no. 33.

Goldsbrough, D.J., 1981, International trade of multinational corporations and its responsiveness to changes in aggregate demand and relative prices, *IMF Staff Papers*, no. 3, pp. 573-599.

Group of Thirty, 1984, *Foreign direct investment 1973-1987*, New York, pp. 23 ff.

Grubel, H.B. and P.J. Lloyd, 1975, *Intra-industry trade: The theory and measurement of international trade in differentiated products*, Wiley, New York.

Hier en Nu, 1981, Radio news commentary, February 18.

IMF, 1977, *Balance of Payments Manual,* 4th edition.

Intermagazine, 1985, nr. 11, November.

Intermediair, 1985, nr. 34, August 23.

Intermediair, 1985, nr. 43, October 25.

Jong, H.W. de, 1985, De internationalisatie van het Nederlandse bedrijfsleven, in: *Ondernemen in Nederland,* Kluwer, Deventer.

Kravis, J.B. en R.E. Lipsey, 1982, The location of overseas production and production for export by US multinational firms, *Journal of International Economics,* no. 12.

Lewis, C., 1948, *The United States and foreign investment problems,* The Brookings Institution.

Mortensen, J. 1984, Rentabiliteit, relatieve factorprijzen en substitutie kapitaal/arbeid in de Gemeenschap, de Verenigde Staten en Japan - 1960/1983, *Europese Economie,* July.

The Netherlands Chamber of Commerce in the United States, 1983, *Results of a survey of Dutch investors that have established operations in the United States.*

Nieuwkerk, M. van, N.P. Driesprong and A.C.J. Stokman, 1982, Aspecten van de Nederlandse betalingsbalans, *Economisch Statistische Berichten* 67, nr. 3381, November 17.

Nieuwkerk, M. van, N.P. Driesprong and H. Lub, 1984, External security transactions of the Netherlands, *Reprint No. 118,* De Nederlandsche Bank N.V.

Pelkmans, J., 1984, *Market integration in the European Community,* The Hague.

Rijksuniversiteit Utrecht, Geografisch Instituut, 1984, *Internationale ondernemingen in Nederland, omvang en lokatie van vestigingen in Nederland,* December.

Stopford, J.M. and J.H. Dunning, 1983, *Multinationals, company performance and global trends,* London.

US Department of Commerce (BEA), 1980, *Foreign direct investment in the United States,* Table 9.

Wellink, A.H.E.M., 1985, Netherlands exporters and international competition, *Quarterly Bulletin 1985/1,* De Nederlandsche Bank N.V.

Whitman, M. v. N., 1981, International trade and investment: two perspectives, *Essays in International Finance,* no. 143, Princeton, New Jersey, July.